THEOLOGY IN THE CITY

THEOLOGY IN THE CITY

A Theological Response to *Faith in the City*

edited by

ANTHONY HARVEY

BP 45 015

First published in Great Britain 1989
SPCK
Holy Trinity Church
Marylebone Road
London NW1 4DU

001454

British Library Cataloguing in Publication Data

Theology in the city.
  1. England. Urban region. Inner areas.
  Society. Role of Church of England 2.
  England. Urban areas. Social conditions.
  Christian viewpoints.
  I. Harvey, Anthony, *1930–* II. Archbishop of
  Canterbury's Commission on Urban Priority
  Areas. Faith in the city
  261.1'0942

  ISBN 0-281-04417-1

Photoset and printed in Great Britain by
WBC Print Ltd, Bristol

Contents

Foreword

Faith in the City made a considerable impact upon the Church and the country at large at the time of its publication. Since then, its influence has been discerned most easily at a practical level. In every city and diocese there have been new policies and initiatives that bear witness to it. But that Report was also theological. One substantial chapter was devoted entirely to theological priorities, and the others showed an awareness of the connection between the practical steps that needed to be taken and the Christian thinking that ought to underlie them.

The authors did not claim to put forward either a new or indeed a complete 'theology of the City'. They believed that this was the task of those whose lives are spent in cities, and indeed there are signs that such a theology is already developing. Meanwhile, they suggested some lines of theological thinking which might help the growth of an authentic 'urban theology'. Their work was an invitation to other theologians to pursue these questions further.

This book is a response to that invitation. Its authors were chosen for the wide range of their interests and experience – liberation theology, black theology and Jewish theology among them – and each has carried the argument forward in his own way. I hope that these essays will be read by many who care for the mission and service of the Church in the great urban centres of this land, and that it will stimulate fresh and urgent theological thinking such as is still required if the impetus given by *Faith in the City* is to be sustained by well-founded Christian convictions.

Robert Cantuar:
December 1988

The Contributors

Dan Cohn-Sherbok is a Rabbi, and is Director of the Centre for the Study of Religion and Society at the University of Kent at Canterbury.

Andrew Hake is an Anglican priest, and was formerly Social Development Officer, Borough of Thamesdown, and a member of the Archbishop's Commission on Urban Priority Areas.

Anthony Harvey was a Lecturer in Theology at the University of Oxford, and is now a Canon of Westminster. He was a member of the Archbishop's Commission on Urban Priority Areas.

Andrew Kirk is an Anglican priest who has spent twelve years of his ministry in South America. He is now Theologian Missioner with the Church Missionary Society and a founder member of the London Institute for Contemporary Christianity, now part of Christian Impact.

Barney Pityana was Vicar of Immanuel Church, Highters Heath, Birmingham, and is now Director of the World Council of Churches Programme to Combat Racism.

Raymond Plant is Professor in the Department of Politics, Southampton University.

Haddon Willmer is a Baptist, and is Tutor of post-graduate students in the Department of Theology and Religious Studies, University of Leeds.

Introduction: An Alternative Theology?

Anthony Harvey

Faith in the City, the Report of the Archbishop of Canterbury's Commission on Urban Priority Areas, claimed to be 'A Call for Action', and the greater part of it was indeed practical and (excessively, its critics would say) pragmatic. Nevertheless its authors believed that their primary task was theological. One chapter – a crucial one – is exclusively theological; and certain theological presuppositions are apparent throughout the rest of the book.

What then was this 'theology'? It has been widely criticized as 'weak', 'inadequate' and 'incoherent'. And certainly it failed to offer a theological scheme or system – a 'theology of the city' – from which a clear practical policy could be deduced. But in fact its authors believed themselves to be doing something more radical and (in the present context) more constructive. They were asking questions about the nature of 'theology' itself, and suggesting that there may be an 'alternative theology' more appropriate to the needs of Urban Priority Areas (and indeed of Christians in many other places) than the theology which has traditionally been taught in our institutions and which has been regarded as the only legitimate way of giving intellectual expression to the Christian faith. Precisely what form this 'theology' might take was not a question they sought to answer: it was one for 'local theologians' to wrestle with themselves. Their concern was simply to suggest the possibility of such an alternative, and to encourage those who might be exploring it. They wrote,

> We see our task more as that of indicating the scope and the constraints within which such theologies can be explored in the Church of today, and to give every possible encouragement to those who are working out their own 'model' or 'theology' in the particular circumstances of their own ministry and vocation.[1]

But this raises a fundamental question. 'Theology' is a recognized discipline, a way of organizing our knowledge and our understanding of God. We are used to different schools, methods and denominational emphases in theology – scholastic, critical, Lutheran etc. In what sense can one legitimately speak of 'theologies' in the plural? Is an 'alternative theology' (such as some of the authors in this book will be arguing for) a logical possibility?

1

It might seem wise to begin still further back and ask, What, in any case, is 'theology'? But rather than try to answer this question directly (which would pre-judge the question with which we are concerned, namely whether it makes sense to talk of 'theologies' rather than just 'theology'), we may start by observing that theological statements claim to be *true*. They do not belong to the realms of poetry, fiction and imagination (though, faced with the ultimate mystery of God, they may have to resort to approximation and even paradox). They are propositions which expose themselves to judgement: are they true or false, meaningful or nonsensical? Philosophers would suggest two main grounds on which a proposition may be held to be true: it may correspond to the observable facts; or it may be logically consistent with other propositions which are held to be true. These two models for propositional truth ('correspondence' and 'coherence') are well exemplified in theology. Just as the truth of the statement 'My aunt died yesterday' can be established by showing that the event it reports did in fact take place as reported, so the truth of the statement 'Christ died under Pontius Pilate' can be established if it can be shown beyond reasonable doubt that the original event corresponds to the subsequent report of it. The particular record of certain crucial past events which theologians call 'revelation' offers a large number of such events or facts, and an important part of the theological enterprise (at least in modern, 'critical', times) has been to establish how far these facts or events 'correspond' to the reports of them contained in Scripture. But theology is about God; and a great many things need to be said about God which can neither be observed nor recorded: we cannot have empirical evidence as to whether God 'corresponds' with all the statements we make about him. A very large number of theological propositions, therefore, must claim to be true by virtue of their coherence and consistency with other propositions. This indeed has been the nature of theological activity in the Church for the greater part of its history. The great christological controversies of the patristic period, for example, were not concerned to establish the truth of statements about the nature of Christ by reference to recorded episodes in his life; they proceeded rather by systematic exploration of all the logical implications of any definition of his nature. Only those could be true which could be shown to be consistent with certain very general propositions about God and Christ which were already agreed by all to be true. One way, therefore, of expressing the familiar axiom that Christian doctrine is based on both reason and revelation would be to say that theological propositions are claimed to be true by virtue of both coherence and correspondence.

It is of course in virtue of their truth by correspondence that in modern times Christian propositions have been most vigorously attacked; the very possibility of reliable knowledge of the historical 'things concerning Jesus' has been called into question. At present there is probably more resistance to this attack, on historical and critical grounds, than was the case a few decades ago. Our knowledge of the 'facts' of biblical history has turned out to be less vulnerable to scientific examination than was once feared. Nevertheless, the prospect that the basic correspondence of Christian propositions with historically verifiable facts might legitimately be called into question caused theologians to ask seriously whether the truth of Christianity might not be maintained without it. The point had been made forcibly by Kierkegaard in his famous assertion,

> If the contemporary generation had left behind them nothing but these words, 'We have believed that in such and such a year God appeared among us in the humble form of a servant, that he lived and taught in our community, and finally died,' it would be more than enough.[2]

And it has in recent years been reiterated not only by existentialist theologians such as Bultmann, but by Maurice Wiles, for example, when he wrote that 'it is essential that the doctrinal theologian recognizes . . . that the kind of information about Jesus that theology has so often looked to the New Testament scholars to provide is not available.'[3] The effect of this is to shift the balance still further away from the correspondence model of truth towards the coherence model. Christian propositions are now more likely to be judged true because they are logically consistent with other propositions and form part of a coherent system than because they correspond with facts or events that can be reliably ascertained from Scripture. Hence the highly significant name of a crucial theological discipline: *systematic theology*. The test to be applied to any theological proposition or doctrine is not whether it corresponds with some recorded or observable reality, but whether it fits into the system.

We need not spend time on the historical reasons for the dominance of this kind of theology for many centuries in the West. Certainly it was the rediscovery (through Latin translations of existing Arabic versions) of some of the works of Aristotle in the twelfth century that provided the tools for constructing a *summa* – a logically coherent system that could claim to articulate the whole Christian religion; and since that time there is no doubt that the standard model for theological reflection has been the systematic refinement of theological propositions. Certain consequences follow from seeing the matter in this way.

First, every proposition that is correctly inserted into the structure of belief must be true by virtue of being logically consistent with the whole. It offers, therefore, a particle of *knowledge*; and progress in the Christian religion then comes to resemble the pursuit of any other learned or scientific enterprise. The further you go, the more you *know*: and the proficiency of the Christian comes to be measured by academic criteria. You cannot be a good Christian unless you 'know' the principal truths of the Christian religion. And the main qualification for ordination in the Church of England, as in many other Churches, is the ability to pass an examination in theology.

A second consequence of the systematic model is that there is no room for more than one system. Diversity of belief becomes a logical impossibility. If the only Christian propositions which are true are those which are logically consistent with all other received propositions, then anyone who holds a belief that is incompatible with the system must be in error. In the Middle Ages this was dealt with simply by treating dissentients as heretics or schismatics. If the propositions they believed could be shown to be inconsistent with the system, then they could have no place in the company of believers and must be excluded or eliminated. At the Reformation this principle came under strain, in that it was no longer a matter of isolated propositions, but a whole series – a sub-system – which was found to be incompatible. But in fact the Reformers never claimed to be establishing an entire alternative system, but rather to be correcting areas of the existing one; and it has been felt uneasily ever since (and particularly in modern times) that there is something inherently sinful in the coexistence of doctrines that are logically irreconcilable, and that 'Christian unity' can be achieved only when a single system has been restored, capable of guaranteeing the truth of all its individual parts.

These two consequences have important implications for the possibility of a 'theology' appropriate to Urban Priority Areas. The assimilation of theological reflection to the acquisition of knowledge has stamped an academic character on church life. Even though there has been a growth in recent years in experience-based exploration of the faith (in counselling and group work among both clergy and lay people), ministers are still accredited mainly in virtue of having attained certain academic standards; lay people are invited to deepen their faith by following courses of study with a conventional academic syllabus; children are 'catechized' in a way they associate with the learning of a 'subject' at school. Working-class people whose education and occupation have given them no taste or aptitude for this kind of intellectual enterprise naturally react against such a presentation of the life of faith (or, if they do not, they may see it as an opportunity for 'bettering themselves' educationally); and those who minister to them are not well prepared by the kind of training they have received to explore fundamentally different ways. As for the unitary character of the theological system – the fact that theological propositions appear to receive their truth by virtue of their consistency with others within a single logically articulated framework – it appears to preclude the possibility of the question we are asking. An 'alternative theology' is a contradiction in terms!

Fortunately, however, this way of seeing and doing theology no longer holds the field unchallenged. Indeed it has come under attack over a wide front, highly theoretical at one end and severely practical at the other. On the theoretical level, it has become clear that the relationship between any theological system and the truth about God is a good deal more problematical than used to be thought. It can be suggested, for example, that theological principles are not necessarily indicators of reality: they may be more like grammatical rules, governing the use of a particular kind of language.[4] Take, for example, some typical trinitarian statements – 'God the Father who created us, God the Son who redeemed us, God the Holy Spirit who sanctifies us.' The persons of the Trinity are 'One God'; so it might be thought that they would be interchangeable as subjects of a sentence. But if someone says that the Holy Spirit redeemed us, or that the Son created us, we have to object. Yet what we object to is not so much that these statements are *untrue*. It is rather that they are *incorrect*. The 'grammar' of theological discourse does not permit us to make them in this form. This does not mean, of course, that theological statements do not describe or point to reality. It does not follow that what we call theology is merely a 'language game'. But it does mean that, just as the same object (which is real, 'out there') can be correctly and truthfully described in French as well as in English, so there may be nothing illogical in suggesting that more than one theological language could be used to describe God, and that each might have its own distinctive 'grammar'. Along this line of thought, there need be no difficulty about the idea of an 'alternative theology'.

This is of course no more than one possible 'model' for understanding the relationship of theological propositions to that ultimate reality which is God. Indeed, in many ways it is an unsatisfactory one, for it does not help us to establish how far the grammatical structure of our theological discourse corresponds with anything in the nature of God himself: it could be the case that we have constructed a 'language' which, though consistent in itself, completely fails to make contact with the reality of God. In fact, however, there may be grounds for taking a more positive view. There is an interesting analogy in the way in which abstract mathematical formulations appear so often to correspond to the way the physical world actually *is*. John Polkinghorne writes:

Mathematics is the free invention of the human mind. Our pure mathematical friends sit in their studies and think their abstract thoughts . . . Yet some of the most intricate patterns they evolve prove to be just those realized in the physical structure of the world . . . There is this remarkable congruence between our inward thought and the outward way things are.[5]

A similar 'congruence' may be held to manifest itself between the highly intellectualized concept of God devised by theologians and the way God actually is: God appears to have acted, and still to act, in ways which conform to the principles or 'rules' of correct theological discourse. But just as no one would say that all mathematical formulae describe patterns that actually exist in the physical world, or that mathematics is the only way to describe that world, so it may be unreasonable to claim that all 'true' theological propositions correspond to the reality of God, or that a single theological system offers the only valid way of talking about him.

Other possible 'models' are suggested by recent developments in the theory of knowledge. Until a relatively short time ago philosophy posed the question of our knowledge of reality in a simple form: How does a human being (the subject) acquire knowledge of the external world (the object)? Is it entirely through perception (empiricism), or through an innate mental structure (rationalism), or some combination of the two? But philosophers would now recognize that subject and object are not so clearly separated. Just as in sub-atomic physics it is realized that the observer 'disturbs' the reality he is observing and so becomes a factor in the observation, so in knowledge generally the data acquired become part of the equipment of the inquirer and are a factor in determining the 'shape' of the reality which is perceived.[6] 'Knowing', in fact, is not so much a foray by the subject into the territory of the object as a conversation between subject and object such that each is modified by contact with the other. Such a model has a striking resonance when it comes to our knowledge of God; for the God of the Bible is often presented as one who, far from being a remote reality towards which human inquiry sends out its probes, is constantly in dialogue with his people; indeed the conversation is one in which God himself, through his Spirit, is actually present in the subject as well as the object (1 Cor. 2.11–12).

It follows from this model that our knowledge of God is unlikely to be capable of being encapsulated in a system of eternally true propositions: the very activity of inquiring into reality exposes us to the disturbance which that reality may cause in our patterns of thought. In *We Believe in God*[7] a further analogy was explored, that of the replacement of Newtonian physics by quantum physics. Further observation of the physical universe since Newton's time revealed phenomena which could not be fitted into his system. A new 'model' or 'paradigm' was needed; but this did not make the Newtonian model incorrect or obsolete. For certain purposes it remains valid, and is in fact the basis of a great deal of our practical engagement with the physical world. But to account for *all* phenomena now observed, a new model was required, which was barely compatible with the old; and we can expect further 'paradigm shifts' in the future. These models, though logically incompatible, can perfectly well coexist: they account for reality seen from different perspectives, and so do not contradict each other. On this analogy, there need be no difficulty in the idea of an 'alternative theology': our constantly enlarging experience and understanding of God, who is a reality greater even than the universe, must be expected to require an occasional 'paradigm shift' which will not necessarily invalidate old doctrines but will open up the possibility of new patterns of systematic thought.

It is not the case, of course, that systematic theology has ever held the field unchallenged as the only means of gaining knowledge of God. There is a long tradition in theology, particularly in the Orthodox tradition, to the effect that God by his very nature so greatly transcends our limited powers of understanding that every statement we make about him must be at most partially true, and will contain a measure of falsity or error: the only valid theological propositions are those which state what God is *not*. Recently John Macquarrie[8] has attempted to bring this into line with Western theological thinking by proposing a model of 'dialectic': if two theological propositions are logically incompatible, this does not mean that one is true and one is false, but that both may have a part of the truth and they may continue in dialectical tension with one another until further advances in knowledge have achieved a synthesis. If accepted, this would provide a further legitimation for the notion of an 'alternative theology': this could be an entire system logically incompatible with the accepted one but standing in a dialectical relationship to it such that it too could claim to offer an account of the truth about God. But in fact the protest against the monopoly of the truth about God held by systematic theology has deeper and more practical roots. Academic theology has of course recognized the importance of prayer and the moral life in the search for the knowledge of God, and has assigned to them the sub-disciplines of 'ascetic' and 'moral' theology. But these sub-disciplines were fashioned after the manner of the primary discipline of systematic theology; and since their subject-matter tended to be too diverse and untidy to fit neatly into an intellectual system, they have been less influential over the living and praying of ordinary Christians than official doctrinal formulations have been over their believing, and have seemed to have considerably less importance in theological studies than the parent disciplines of biblical and systematic theology. And yet from early times a succession of Christian thinkers has insisted on the *priority* of moral and spiritual effort over academic inquiry. Irenaeus wrote, 'It is better to know little or nothing and so to come close to God through love than to acquire much knowledge . . . and be found a blasphemer and enemy of God.'9 The author of *The Imitation of Christ* wrote, 'I would rather have contrition than be able to define it.'10 And this shift of priorities away from theoretical speculation is not confined to the Christian religion: in Islam there has always been a distrust of academic discussion about the nature of God on the grounds that it is a distraction from the more serious business of attending to God's commands.

This last point brings us closer to those vigorous protests against the dominance of Western academic theology which have been raised in recent years – liberation theology, black theology, feminist theology and various forms of 'local theology'. It has been tempting for theologians trained in traditional Western theology to assume that these movements could be understood in much the same way as one has talked in the past of 'German theology' or 'British theology': it is assumed that theology is still one basic discipline; all that is new is that new people are doing it – oppressed people in Latin America, black people, women, local people. If they come up with conclusions at variance with the tradition, this may be because they work in a somewhat different idiom and ask themselves somewhat different questions. But ultimately the truth and validity of their theology must be tested, like all theological propositions, by its correspondence with the data of revelation and its coherence with the established system of doctrine (this is indeed precisely how the Sacred Congregation for the Doctrine of the Faith has attempted to form an authoritative judgement on liberation theology). But now, given that we have opened up the theoretical possibility of 'alternative theologies', we have to ask whether these names may not be more than simply a sociological indicator. Do they denote something which may be called a 'theology' in its own right?

One might be tempted to try to answer this question by passing each of these 'theologies' under review and examining their credentials. Does each or any of them give an adequate account of the Christian faith? But to respond in this way is to assume that we have some criterion by which to judge whether any theology is 'adequate', and such a criterion could only be theological and its validity would depend on that particular 'theology' from which it is derived. Traditional

INTRODUCTION: AN ALTERNATIVE THEOLOGY?

Western theologians will inevitably apply a criterion derived from 'systematic theology', whereas it is precisely the validity of this criterion which is challenged by, for example, liberation theologians when they claim that a theological proposition is fully 'true' only when it is also 'truly liberating'. Moreover, sociologists of knowledge would insist that Western theology itself has been as much conditioned by 'non-theological factors' as any of its contemporary competitors. Its practitioners having been mainly members of the educated, economically secure and relatively leisured classes, its interests have been primarily intellectual and it has been ready to accept as 'true' even theological propositions that permitted such manifestly unchristian activities as the Inquisition, the amassing of wealth by the Church, or the persecution of the Jews. It is no longer possible to claim that the Western theological tradition necessarily offers a superior criterion by which the claims of other 'theologies' can be judged.

In point of fact, the testing of any theology, including the 'academic' theology of the Western Churches, is a more complex and long-term matter than simply setting certain propositions against a grid provided by reason and revelation. The Church of England Doctrine Commission's Report, *Believing in the Church*,[11] attempted to spell out this process, and described it less as an academic examination in which certain answers are judged correct or false but rather as a continuous conversation between theologians, bishops, priests, congregations, liturgists and hymn-writers. Doctrine is never a static thing that can be set down on paper in a form adequate for this generation and the next; it is the fruit of a continuing enterprise by all members of the Church, according to their differing gifts and capacities, to fashion their lives according to the commands of the gospels, amid the conditions of the world of today, in the fellowship of the Church. Doctrinal formations, the language of worship, the evolution of moral attitudes, the study of Scripture, all interact with one another continuously. An essential part of this process is 'theology' itself. But the adequacy of this theology is constantly tested in the living and praying of the Church, which in turn influences the next generation of theologians.

It follows that no single system of theology is in a position to pass judgement on another 'theology'. The testing will take place within the Church or Christian community where that theology has taken root, and that Church or community in turn will enter into a conversation with the wider Church, a conversation by which both partners may eventually be influenced, so that the doctrine of neither may be the same at the end as it was in the beginning, but either may exert a challenging or a moderating influence on the other. All these Churches or communities are of course claiming to remain faithful to the historic

9

tradition of the faith based on the Scriptures; but the manner in which they do so may vary widely (from the fundamentalist to the liberal, to take only the most obvious example), and no single theological tradition is in a position to pass judgement on the faithfulness of all the others. Moreover, the ultimate objective of unity between Churches or denominations is no longer expressed in terms of complete doctrinal agreement. Phrases such as 'the pluralism of typologies within ecclesial allegiance' are now currently used by ecumenical theologians. It is becoming increasingly recognized that a diversity of forms of expression of Christian truth, far from being sinful and temporary, is in fact inherent in the Christian religion,[12] just as there has for centuries been a legitimate difference of conviction over a practical matter as central as that of the proper Christian attitude to the use of force and the bearing of arms.

Along these lines, I believe it is possible to make out a case for the validity of a 'local theology'[13] which may be very different in style and content from the theological discipline in which up to now virtually all ministers and teachers in the Church of England have been trained and which most lay people assume offers the standard programme for Christian proficiency. It can also be argued that the testing of any such theology should properly take place in the locality itself, though still within the wider fellowship of the Church; traditional theological disciplines do not provide criteria which can be applied to theological activity that has adopted a different model for the articulation of Christian truth. But this does not mean there can be no contact between the two. Indeed it is essential that a dialogue should be maintained. The lack of any such dialogue is only too apparent in the case of liberation theology and of black and feminist theology, where the use made of the Bible, for example, is often frankly pre-critical or fundamentalist. Traditionally trained theologians should be ready to assist in the development and monitoring of a local theology, and at the same time to be challenged by the new methods and insights which arise from it. The possibilities and limitations of this dialogue will be known only when it has got under way; but in the meantime it is possible to observe certain recent developments in academic theology itself which offer at least a bridgehead to those 'alternative theologians' who may attempt to engage in serious conversation:

Narrative theology. Claims have been made by academic theologians themselves that this is a genuinely new theological idiom capable of expressing the nature of the God of the Bible – a God who is active, personal and involved in human history – better than any system of timeless propositions. It places great emphasis on the narrative component in Scripture, and suggests that the appropriate response to this narrative material is not to try to extract general propositions from it but rather to bring it into relationship with the 'stories' of our own lives and our own society, and to encourage any kind of narration and dramatization which helps this process to take place. Many scholars now believe that these claims are exaggerated: the alleged primacy of narrative over propositions, whether historically or theoretically, is open to question, and the necessary task of discerning between 'stories' that are theologically either true or false seems to require tools that cannot be furnished by the study of 'narrative' itself. Nevertheless, narrative theology has been successful in drawing attention to the undoubted devaluation which traditional theology has imposed on the 'story material' of Scripture, and can give legitimate encouragement to local theologians who find a greater response among lay people to narrative and drama than to traditional doctrinal teaching.

The Jewish tradition. It was only in response to the challenge of Christian systematic theology that any comparable 'Jewish theology' emerged – the first was written in the nineteenth century and was the work of a Christian theologian! The Jewish tradition, working on the Hebrew Scriptures it shared with Christian theology, nevertheless followed an entirely different path. It was concerned not with indicative propositions, but with imperatives. Given the law of God, as revealed in the biblical commandments, how could these be applied to the various situations of daily life, which was now often lived under conditions never envisaged by the biblical authors? These questions gave rise to the immense body of authoritative *halakha* (which Christians have been inclined to regard, somewhat dismissively, as casuistry) which stands at the heart of all Jewish 'theologizing'. It is a discipline demanding great subtlety and rigour (some of its principles, indeed, are often thought to have been derived from Aristotelian logic), and a mastery of it is possible only for highly trained minds. But its conclusions take the form of highly specific and practical rules of conduct, of which the relevance is immediately seen by any lay person in a way which is not the case, for example, in Christian teaching on the Trinity. Now certainly the notion of a Christian *halakha* presents difficulties: most of the Old Testament precepts on which it might be based are (for a Christian) obsolete, and the Christian 'law of love' is hardly amenable to the precise distinctions of jurists. Yet it must be said that for many people (perhaps particularly those in the Urban Priority Areas) the word 'Christian' stands primarily for a type of conduct or moral attitude, and if asked to elaborate on this they will offer anecdote and example rather than a chain of inference from the doctrine of the atonement. At least it could be said that a 'popular theology' might a have a stronger '*halakhic*' character than the usually received theology, and that this would have a significant parallel in the Jewish 'theological tradition', which itself rests on part of the same biblical revelation.

Syllabus demarcation. All theologians are trained in a set of distinct disciplines: Bible, doctrine, church history, moral theology and so forth. These distinctions date back only to the Renaissance, and, however convenient, are clearly artificial; but once theological study has been organized in these categories for a period of centuries it becomes difficult to imagine doing the subject in any other way. Consequently any Christians who wish to deepen their understanding of the faith are liable to be confronted with a course of study arranged in a syllabus designed to cover these separate areas. One consequence of this has been that even clergy have often found themselves badly equipped to tackle a moral or religious issue of contemporary importance by drawing on the resources of the Christian tradition: their training may have enabled them to say something about the biblical, doctrinal or historical background to the subject, but they have little skill in bringing together relevant material from all these disciplines and working towards an answer that is genuinely the distillation of the Christian tradition as a whole. And for lay people (particularly those who have not received a higher education) there is the daunting prospect that all these disciplines have to be in some sense 'covered' before they can do any real Christian thinking at all.

It is not easy for theologians trained according to the traditional syllabus to imagine any other way of doing it. But the educational emphasis of the last few decades on 'beginning where people are' has made it an urgent matter to find ways of starting with situations that occur in people's lives and working them out in the light of any part of the Christian tradition that may be relevant to them. This is a procedure which has often been attempted in lay theological education but has usually broken down in face of the immense conventional pressure to concentrate on 'subjects' rather than 'topics', to acquire knowledge before you can apply it. But there seems no reason in principle why theology should not be studied (as it were) thematically rather than according to a syllabus, other than the very natural disinclination of the teachers to teach in a way totally different from that in which they have received their own training. If so, then it could be expected that a theology 'local' to an Urban Priority Area might begin with genuinely urban and working-class perceptions and build up a repertory of resources from all parts of the Christian tradition which would in effect become the theological equipment of these local 'theologians' in the same way (though, one might hope, also in a more effective way) as traditionally trained ministers are equipped with a smattering of Bible, doctrine, history, ethics and liturgy.[14] Academic theologians would still have a role in ensuring that this repertory was as full and balanced as possible, and that this form of theological reflection was pursued with discipline and rigour (and this in turn would present a formidable and challenging programme of academic training). But they could do this adequately only if they gained some experience of the method themselves; and it could then even happen (and this is part of the challenge to traditional theology mentioned at the beginning) that the thematic method of this local theology could begin to have a reciprocal and wholesome effect on academic theological education itself.

These three examples are no more than pointers to developments in recent academic theology that may offer new opportunities for dialogue with an 'alternative theology'. What this alternative theology might be is a question which is explored (from one point of view) in Chapter 1. The purpose of this Introduction has been simply to argue for the theoretical legitimacy of such a theology, and to give reasons why it is important, indeed urgent, that all theologians should attend to it and welcome it. Any real 'faith in the city' demands a readiness to listen, not only to practical initiatives, but to any theological methods and insights that may be an authentic expression of Christian life and witness in Urban Priority Areas.

Notes

1 The Archbishop's Commission on Urban Priority Areas, *Faith in the City* (Church House Publishing, 1985), 3.44.
2 S. Kierkegaard, *Philosophical Fragments*, tr. D. F. Swenson (Princeton University Press, 1936), p. 87.
3 M. Wiles, *The Remaking of Christian Doctrine* (SCM Press, 1974), p. 48.
4 See G. A. Lindbeck, *The Nature of Doctrine* (SPCK, 1985).
5 J. Polkinghorne, *One World* (SPCK, 1986), pp. 45-6.
6 See the discussion of M. Polanyi in C. Gunton, *Enlightenment and Alienation* (Marshall, Morgan & Scott, 1985), pp. 37-44.
7 The Doctrine Commission of the Church of England, *We Believe in God* (Church House Publishing, 1987), pp. 22-5.
8 J. Macquarrie, *In Search of Deity* (SCM Press, 1984).
9 Irenaeus, *Adv. Haer.*, 2.26.1.
10 Thomas à Kempis, *The Imitation of Christ*, 1.1.

11 The Doctrine Commission of the Church of England, *Believing in the Church* (SPCK, 1981).
12 See S. Sykes, *The Identity of Christianity* (SPCK, 1984). J. D. G. Dunn, *Unity and Diversity in the New Testament* (SCM Press, 1977), illustrates the existence of 'alternative' theologies in New Testament times.
13 Other arguments are used by R. J. Schreiter, who reaches similar conclusions in his *Constructing Local Theologies* (SCM Press, 1985).
14 I am indebted for this suggestion to Professor J. L. Houlden. See his *Connections* (SCM Press, 1986), ch. 4. This is in fact the pattern of 'doing theology' in base communities promoted by liberation theology. See below, Chapter 1.

1

A Different Task:
Liberation Theology
and Local Theologies

Andrew Kirk

INTRODUCTION

Contrary to a number of comments on *Faith in the City*, the Report was not weak on theology. That its theological reflection tended to be somewhat tentative and provisional is due both to the issues under review, namely inner-city deprivation and the Church's response, and to the present state of play in the Western tradition of theology.

What critics may have wanted to see was some kind cf systematic theological reflection on such topics as the nature of human life, justice and injustice, reconciliation and salvation, starting from a firm base in Christian doctrine. What they did find was the beginning of a re-evaluation of the theological task as such. This kind of programme follows from the conviction that, if the Church is going to clarify the nature of its calling in relation to social and human decay in Britain today, the Christian community at all levels is required to look afresh at the way it thinks about the significance of its God-given faith.

For a number of reasons (which I have presented in full elsewhere[1]), traditional Western theology is ill-equipped to provide the resources for a sustained consideration of the ways in which the Christian gospel should interact with concrete social, political and economic realities. Basically, it has not learnt how to engage hermeneutically with the relationship between revealed faith and the network of opinions, structures and patterns of life which make up our kind of society.[2] Therefore, the Report is right, I believe, to suggest that 'It is time for the Church to recognize that the priorities for theological study and education need not always be set by the prescriptions of a traditional academic syllabus and to give every encouragement to the growth of theologies that are authentic expressions of local cultures.'[3]

Recognizing the vital contribution already made by liberation and other Third World theologies to the fulfilment of this hope, I would like to try to explore in this chapter some of the implications and possibilities of doing theology which makes full use of the gifts and experiences of ordinary Christian people. First, though, I will try to

15

substantiate my comments on the inadequacy of the present theological endeavour to meet the demands of the Church seeking to rediscover its God-directed purpose at the margins of our kind of society.

A CRITIQUE OF THE ACADEMIC TRADITION OF THEOLOGY

One of the major weaknesses of the current academic approach to theology is a failure to deal critically enough with its own assumptions. In particular, the methods, agenda and purpose of theology have all remained largely unquestioned by the community of professionals, as if there was a tacit agreement that the price of admittance to the guild of scholars was a commitment not to break ranks. Academic theology has tended to be too uncritical of its starting-point in radical scepticism. Also it has not faced the challenge that the context in which it is done, a context which abstracts intellectual work from the whole of life and the theoretical from the practical, actually distorts the task. Sometimes scholars have broken ranks in terms of particular theories (e.g. whether Jesus was a Zealot or not), but hardly at all concerning the belief that the ultimately normative way of doing and verifying theology is that practised and perfected in Western centres of learning.

Radical dissent over the nature of the theological task, then, has been remarkably sparse within the Western theological world, and largely marginalized. It has, however, come forcefully from people belonging to cultures beyond the Euro-American centre.

Liberation and allied theologies make a point of highlighting and defending the particular perspectives from which their reflection comes. They believe that theological thought has no option but to make a virtue out of a necessity, for both the methods and content of theology arise from one kind of commitment or another. A disinterested neutrality in approaching the texts and the demands that they make on faith is literally impossible. It is disingenuous of scholars, therefore, to pretend that they can offer an unbiased, methodologically objective, body of knowledge in the areas of biblical study and systematic theology which can then be applied, according to circumstances, to Christian social, pastoral and ethical thinking and action. Interaction between a theologian's background and culture and intellectual work takes place at the point of the elaboration of his or her ideas, and not only when they are applied. That is why hermeneutics is the paramount issue for the theological task, a fact not yet fully taken on board by Western theology.

The reality is that from their training, their cultural background and their own inclinations regarding belief scholars have adopted a

16

number of presuppositions which colour both the methods and the results of their investigations. This may not be so obvious in disciplines like textual criticism or grammatical analysis, but becomes patently so when scholars engage in textual and theological reconstruction according to hypotheses and conjecture based on possible historical constructs. Evidence for these assertions could be given in the case of the 'form-critical' method of analysis of texts and the current tendency to find in the New Testament a mutually independent set of theologies.

Prior commitments are also clearly evident in cases where theological investigation might otherwise produce results which seem to conflict with the prevailing attitudes of the group they most closely identify with. Certain approaches to inter-faith dialogue which seek to modify the highly particular nature of New Testament Christology, and ethical decision-making in the area of social change and political confrontation are current examples of this process.

The existence of a pluralist society in which world-views and value-systems jostle one another for recognition, and in which the acceptance of an equal validity for any beliefs (for reasons of racial and ideological tolerance and harmony) is a high priority, has provoked some people to highlight the plurality, and even the mutual contradiction, of different theological perspectives in the Bible.

It would be surprising indeed if the prevailing relativistic atmosphere of Western culture concerning matters of faith did not produce a vigorous denial, in some theological quarters, of all claims to final truth about God and his human creation. The immediate question at issue here is not whether theologians are right or not to be influenced by these and other manifestations of contemporary culture, but their frequent silence about which assumptions have been accepted and which rejected and their failure to argue cogently in favour of the underlying perspectives adopted. Perhaps, before the real task of theology can begin, there needs to be a 'proto-theological' phase in which people become aware of how past and present socio-cultural factors have shaped theology historically.

The purpose of this discussion is to claim that not only should the task of theological reflection be diversified, but that traditional academic theology should no longer be considered the measure of all authentic theology. It is here that even Anthony Harvey's bold option for alternative models of theology[4] may not be an adequate response to the cultural and sociological critique of the academic style of doing theology. Although he proposes a 'paradigm shift' in theology, in order to allow space for 'local theologies' to arise from real grass-roots involvement in the Church's mission in Urban Priority Areas, he does

17

not see that this brings the currently accepted model into serious doubt.

He speaks of a dialectical relationship and complementary approaches, while admitting that the models may be logically incompatible. It is perhaps not surprising, therefore, that, in spite of a vigorous appeal for freedom to explore new models, he finishes by making academic theology once again a privileged arbiter of the balance of theological content.[5] Of course to talk of a 'paradigm shift' is not to excuse arbitrary and inadequate exegesis of foundational texts. Debate about the original meaning must go on, with no one group claiming a necessary advantage in understanding. The point at issue is not about legitimate interpretation, but about an overall approach to the text which sees the hermeneutical dimension as fundamental.

On the whole, Third World theologies have come to the conclusion that the Western academic model of theology is too tied to the historical development of Western cultural imperialism to serve as a legitimate vehicle of theological reflection that wants to be faithful to the full demands of the gospel. The paradigm shift which the universal Church needs today does not, as a matter of fact, allow incompatible theological methods to stand side by side. Rather, it looks for a different way of authenticating the validity of theological statements. The acceptance of alternative, apparently mutually incongruous, models of doing theology already presupposes the correctness of a plurality of beliefs: that is, it springs directly from one of the basic assumptions of Western culture. For this reason it proposes no really critical principle for modern theology.

Liberation theology, as I understand it, does not accept the kind of plurality which allows traditional theologies to remain fundamentally unchallenged. On the contrary, it finds fault with these theologies in the Western tradition on three main scores. First, theology's responsibility to uncover and express the significance of the gospel has tended to be fulfilled in terms of the search for existential meaning rather than in terms of social and political change. In this way theology has simply reinforced the deeply ingrained individualism of the Western view of life. Second, scholarship has been conducted largely as an end in itself, often to advance an academic career, and therefore much of the research carried out is socially and missiologically irrelevant, but not thereby socially and missiologically neutral. Third, many theological issues are dealt with as if they were largely intellectual questions. As a result, in coming to discern the truth about a situation and the necessary action which is called for, a pre-eminent place is given to rational theories and hypotheses. Applied theology, which deals with matters of direct pastoral and missionary concern, is considered to follow from the application of systematic theology (formed as the result of the interaction of ideas) to practical living.

These criticisms are not about peripheral matters, which a few minor adjustments to the system could take care of. They challenge the very core suppositions of theology as an academic pursuit and put in its place 'a new way of doing theology'.[6]

European theology has tended to consider itself as the highest form of theology (the most sophisticated and rigorous available), demonstrating thereby its captivity to a kind of evolutionary view of 'progress' in theology and to the characteristic drive of Western societies to dominate and prove their superior cultural achievements. One of the major differences between the Western pursuit of theology and theological reflection from the Third World is that the former operates as the power of knowledge over people, while the latter seeks to release the power of God's people from within Christian communities to be agents of transformation.

LIBERATION THEOLOGY DECLARES ITS AIMS

There are at least four major assumptions which liberation theology has no hesitation in highlighting as the springboard for its own understanding of the theological task.

First, theology acts as a critical reflection on the thinking and practice of the Church. One of its functions is to monitor the way power operates within ecclesiastical institutions, determining to a greater or lesser degree their evangelistic and pastoral practice and their explicit or implicit political involvement. It will, therefore, be involved in looking critically at the reasons used to defend particular attitudes and activities and to make pronouncements of one kind or another. For example, it may challenge certain theories of the ordained ministry as little more than ingenious legitimations of a closed, authoritarian style of leadership. Or, it may question why Christian leaders, in certain instances, hesitate so much to make unequivocal statements on specific, grave social abuses (for example, in Britain the community charge, or 'poll tax', which, as proposed, is oppressive because discriminatory against those on low incomes). As Hugo Assmann once forcefully commented, 'Christian churches have so many absolutes, so many certitudes, and yet when it comes to the basic contradictions in the world, they have only humble opinions.'[7]

Second, the historical situation in which the Church finds itself is the starting-point for considering its mission. Some liberation theologians call this the 'first text' or 'book of life', which is the indispensable context for reading and interpreting the 'second text' –

God's Word. Theology, then, becomes critical reflection on the economic and social realities of any particular society in the light of the given Word. Quite simply, theological reflection needs contemporary data to engage with if it is going to be contemporary theology.

The most important aspect of this reality is the endemic nature of poverty, and the complete failure of modern development projects to lessen the gigantic gap which exists between the affluent and the poor. The worsening conditions of the poor should not cause sorrow and pity so much as anger and indignation. Poverty is not only a tragedy, even more it is a scandal, for well-canvassed solutions[8] to problems with clearly definable causes are rejected, not because they would not work, but because of the vested interests that would be threatened.

Theology is a task to be undertaken in solidarity with those who suffer from the refusal of the powerful to change their policies. At the same time, the poor become a category for understanding God and how he acts in the world.

Liberation theology today is tending to emphasize that the task of the professionally trained theologian is to articulate the Christian reflection of the poor. In this context the biblical theologian Carlos Mesters has some provocative remarks to make:

> The example of popular interpretation given shows a deep familiarity with the Bible. It is not the familiarity of someone who knows the Bible from end to end, but that of someone who feels at home with it. Before this renewal movement began the Bible was always something that belonged to those who taught, commanded and paid, and was explained in such a way as to confirm them in the knowledge that enabled them to teach, the power that enabled them to command and the possession of money that enabled them to pay.
>
> Now the Bible is beginning to belong on the side of those who are taught, ordered and paid. They are discovering that there is nothing in the Bible to confirm the others in their knowledge, power and money, which they use to control the impoverished people. . . Despite all its faults and uncertainties, the interpretation of the Bible these people are making can make a great contribution to exegesis itself. The people's contribution is made not through spectacles but through their eyes. The eyes of the people are recapturing the sure vision with which Christians should read and interpret the Bible. So this popular interpretation is a warning to the manufacturers of spectacles – the exegetes. Spectacles have to be made to suit eyes, if vision is to be improved. When eyes have to be adapted to suit spectacles vision is spoiled and the world grows dark.[9]

This quotation underlines one of the basic principles of liberation theology, that gaining knowledge of the truth is dependent upon paying strict attention to the historical circumstances of those looking for it, and in particular their relative status in society. The poor, for two reasons, are in a privileged position to be able to hear and understand the will of the Lord: first, because the Bible largely addresses a message of hope and assurance to people like themselves – there is already a large degree of correspondence between those who heard the original message and those who listen to it today; second, because they have no vested interest in maintaining positions of privilege which resist the strong biblical call to conversion and substantial change.

Third, theology needs to use the social sciences in order to make its reflection concrete. If theology is a missiological enterprise, then it has to grapple with the way societies work, and in particular how economic structures favour particular segments of the population and work to the disadvantage of others. In other words, theology has to take on board a structural analysis of economic systems and political institutions.

Liberation theology has largely accepted the Marxist critique of capitalism as a correct way of explaining the increasing inequality between an owning class of people and those who possess nothing but their labour to sell, and who are dependent on a job-market which is manipulated in the interests of depressing wages and curbing the power of working people to organize themselves. Nationally and internationally the economic order is designed to preserve the untrammelled flow of capital and its ability to multiply itself, irrespective of the human misery caused.

Liberation theologians take for granted that the relationship between Marxism and atheism is an accident of history. The denial of God's existence and the ridiculing of religion as 'opium' and 'the halo of this vale of tears' spring from the general humanistic climate which Marx breathed and uncritically endorsed while at university. Atheism is a legacy of the self-consciously rationalistic assumptions of the Enlightenment. It also reflects Marx's rejection of Christian faith, because it was used to support the givenness of inequality in human society, and because he failed to see that in reality faith in the God of Jesus liberates human beings from all forms of alienation and oppression. It is not derived in any direct way from Marx's economic or political analysis, and makes little sense to the poor who look to God to defend their cause against exploitation. Therefore, liberation theologians maintain, it is perfectly possible both to be a theist and to accept the Marxist social interpretation.[10]

Fourth, theology cannot be divorced from ideology. Theologians have to reckon with the fact that social conflict is part and parcel of particular economic and political situations. Marx did not invent the

21

class struggle as an abstract concept, he discovered a real situation pertaining within a given set of social relationships.

Ideology, in its negative sense, is an intellectual construction, derived from certain beliefs and attitudes, which acts to legitimize the vested interests of the groups which hold it. Perverted forms of Christian faith have sometimes been used in an ideological manner to justify the way things are in society.

It is of the essence of the ideological critique that institutions in society cannot remain neutral. The Church, therefore, has to choose on whose side it will deploy its resources in the present social conflicts. All its thinking, structures and activities will reflect this choice. If it takes 'a preferential option for the poor', then all its theological work must be adjusted accordingly, interpreting the Christian faith from the perspective of the outsider. Any other perspective, such as the attempt to conciliate between those possessing power and those who are the victims of it, will be suspected of engaging in ideological collusion. As Leonardo Boff says, 'The theology of liberation attempts to elaborate the whole content of Christianity, beginning from the demands of a social liberation that anticipates and mediates the definitive liberation of the kingdom.'[11]

In general terms we can say that the hard facts of growing destitution and despondency in many nations, now including so-called developed ones, have presented theology with a new agenda, ideological critique with a new way of doing it and the Bible with the ultimate criteria for guaranteeing that the reflection incorporates the unique dimensions of the gospel. Liberation theology has been called a 'political hermeneutic of the gospel'. The purpose of theology is to mediate between political commitment to change society and the sources of the Christian faith.

If radical in a fully biblical sense, theology is bound to be a subversive and polemical activity, arousing hostility in the conservative, liberal and even radical establishments. The rightness of theological reflection cannot be measured ultimately by its conformity to criteria laid down by a professional élite, but by its ability to inspire men and women to costly Christian discipleship in implementing the biblical message of grace and liberation in Jesus Christ.

THEOLOGY AT THE GRASS-ROOTS

We come now to the hardest part of the exercise: the attempt to suggest ways (inspired by the assumptions and methods of liberation theology) in which a genuinely indigenous, contextual theology might take shape within Christian communities rooted in Urban Priority Areas.

Using the four basic assumptions which liberation theology underlines as the key to a valid way of doing theology, I will attempt a few precursory comments on how theology *might* unfold at the frontier of the Church's mission. As there are no real examples yet of genuinely local theologies to discuss, I can only very tentatively suggest possible ways forward. Liberation theology does not provide an easy blueprint. It may, however, inspire imaginative new attempts to reflect theologically on the Church's task in a concrete reality.

Critical reflection on the thinking and practice of the Church

In the first place, then, the local Christian community will take a long, hard look at the Church as an institution at the local, national and global levels. In order to have some raw data as a basis from which to reflect critically, it may want to conduct a survey both among its own members and those who remain outside as to how they view the Church. It will need to pay attention particularly to what people think the Church is for, and how far they think the Church is fulfilling the purpose they have given it.

In the process, they will need to identify elements in the replies which could be said to reflect a popular or 'folk religious' tradition. No doubt they will find underlying the responses a number of assumptions about the role of the Church and religion in general which are important indicators of the inner dynamic of culture: for example, views about prayer, community, moral attitudes, and the private and public dimensions of faith.

It would be easy to dismiss popular attitudes on the grounds that probably they are fairly far removed from the New Testament's presentation of the gospel. However, the effort really to understand the thinking processes and motivating factors in the lives of ordinary people will repay ample dividends, not least because it should help the Christian community discern promising and unproductive bridges for communicating the gospel.

One of the key ways into understanding any culture is to discover how people cope with the significant moments and questions of life. A further survey will perhaps be necessary to allow the local population to tell in its own words what it thinks of family life, how it copes with human differences (for example, male and female roles, ethnic diversity, employed and unemployed, the well-off and those struggling to survive), what its response is to sickness and suffering, success and failure, and, above all, what it thinks life is ultimately all about. In each case it will be important to note implicit or explicit references to religious values, and what place, if any, the Church occupies in the attempt to make sense of life.

A further element in the investigation will be to secure some local opinions, however stereotyped they may appear, about the place and function of the Church at a national level. Here, probably, trenchant views about the Church and its relation to an established order (which it is expected to guarantee and uphold), not to mention its great wealth, may well come to the fore. Convictions about the supposed role of the Church in supporting a power élite in society are difficult to unravel, though they will be held with great force. Specific questions about the Church in a given city like Liverpool, Bradford or Birmingham may elicit comments related more closely to people's own experience.

The local Christian community should be able to collect together a wealth of material which will help it to see where others place the Church in relation to the rest of society. As a second stage in its own reflection, it will want to discern how far these varied opinions suggest changes in the life of the Church. To do this it will need to go first to the 'second text', the pages of the New Testament. Mindful of the fact that some members will not be used to systematic Bible study, or for that matter to reading very much at all, an approach might be to present in spoken, visual and even dramatic form some models of church life in the New Testament. The purpose would be to discover, both from the stories themselves and the comments of the New Testament writers, what the Church is intended to be. The models might be the Church in Jerusalem, as reflected in the early chapters of Acts; the Church in Palestine as seen through the eyes of James; the Church in Corinth as portrayed in 1 Corinthians and, finally, the Church in the Letter to the Ephesians. In each case the local group of Christians would be given every encouragement to share their comments and together draw a profile of the characteristics, right and wrong, of the New Testament Church.

As a further stage in the task of reflecting theologically from where they are, the local Christian community would be invited to relate the two surveys (of popular opinions and of the biblical material) and discuss how, on the basis of its investigation, the life of the Church ought to develop in the future. A final part of this particular process would be for it to commit itself to concrete steps to bring about this development.

This kind of task would be one way of responding creatively to the first assumption of liberation theology. Of course it could also include other components, such as using models of church life from other periods of church history and other parts of the world.

Mission starting from the reality of the poor

In the second place, the Christian community will explore the reality and significance of the poor. In order to vary the approach, a start could be made from the scriptural data. To discover the rich depth of meaning which the different parts of the Bible bring to the poor, a thematic study would have to be undertaken.

Given the limited resources a local congregation in an Urban Priority Area would have, probably they could begin with the use of only a concordance and a cross-reference Bible. This could be amplified later with the use of biblical dictionaries, commentaries and articles specifically on the theme. In this way the group would learn that the basic meaning of being poor (particularly in the Old Testament) is being the object of oppression, but that there are at least 'twenty or more causes of poverty mentioned in the Bible in addition to oppression'.[12] Later they would discover further nuances from the New Testament, particularly the relationship between being poor and the Kingdom of God, poverty as a characteristic of the Messiah, and the oppression of sin, the law, death and Satan.

If they were following the lead from liberation theology, they would want to ask: Up to what point does the Bible present God as 'biased towards the poor'? What implications does it draw from this affirmation? An allied question has to do with the rich: What is God's message to them? If the good news is preached to the poor, does this mean that the rich inevitably hear it as 'bad news', and are thus sent away empty (Luke 1.53)?

When, as an initial step, the community has gathered as much information as it wants to, and has been able to digest it at least in part, it will look for examples in its own neighbourhood of categories of the poor similar to those it has found through reading the Scriptures. It will try to answer the question about the causes of poverty, asking itself how far the category of oppression makes sense in a British Urban Priority Area today.

The Bible speaks not only of material poverty, but also of a poverty characterized by a relationship with God based on trust and hope that evil will be overcome and a new human reality opened up. How far does this attitude pervade the church community, and how far do the poor in high-rise flats, new corporation estates and rented lodgings display a poverty which is marked by a reliance on God?

Liberation theology notes three phases in the Church's concern for the poor. First, when groups of Christians became increasingly involved in living alongside the poorest of the poor (deep inside the shanty towns of the great conurbations), sharing their life, their sorrows and celebrations, the Church was *with* the poor.

Second, from that vantage-point the Church, in sharing not only the life of marginalized people but also their struggles to get their rights

25

recognized, became the Church *for* the poor. It used its resources and influence to counteract the exploitation of the poor by unscrupulous landlords and to bring desperately needed amenities into the localities where disadvantaged people live.

A third, qualitatively different, step has been taken when the Church becomes the Church *of* the poor. No longer does the Church come in from the outside, as it were, as a well-defined body to act on behalf of the poor. They now hear for themselves the good news of Jesus and the Kingdom and seek to translate it into action within their fellowship and beyond in the community. These are the Base Ecclesial Communities.[13]

A locally indigenous theology might well want to explore the reasons for and the implications of these three different relationships between poor people and the Christian community. Such theological themes as incarnation, service, sharing of gifts, partnership and enabling will come under review. A major aspect of the task will be to encourage grass-roots people to discover the resources they possess and to share them with Christians elsewhere. As *Faith in the City* says: 'Our task as a Church is by no means only to show concern for the victims of oppressive social conditions; it is also to find ways of discerning and receiving the gifts of those who have worked out a genuine Christian discipleship under circumstances of "multiple deprivation".'[14]

Making use of social disciplines of analysis and the critique of ideology

The third and fourth assumptions of liberation theology can conveniently be taken together. Thus, in the third place, the Christian community will seek to use in its Christian reflection social and economic studies which set out to explain both the conditions and the causes of life in the Urban Priority Areas.

Whether or not it accepts a broadly Marxist account of inequality and deprivation should depend on how accurately this interpretation of reality explains the recurring problems. The value of the Marxist analysis is that it is not afraid to uncover a fundamental conflict in human relations due to the way economic forces work. It opposes completely the optimistic view, in the tradition of Adam Smith, that free-market forces produce a harmony of economic interests throughout the population.

Marxism starts from a premise of suspicion that in the present economic order the system works in such a way that only some are relatively free to use a largely uncurbed power to benefit themselves. All capitalist societies inherently promote and aggravate a gross inequality in the distribution of resources. They are designed to allow, if not actively to encourage, the private accumulation of capital, which is then defended as the highest economic and social good.

In its purest form capitalism exalts capital over labour. The worker who is hired for a particular job and paid the wage which the market determines is always highly vulnerable. In the interests of profit-maximization and the attraction of share-ownership through the payment of generous dividends, the worker's wages or job are under constant threat.

The power of privately owned capital to determine access to work and the material quality of life, or lack of it, of millions of working-class people has been curtailed in two important ways over the course of time: through progressive taxation wealth has been redistributed in the form of 'free' services – notably education, health care and supplementary payments to ensure a minimum standard of living – and through the legalized power of trade unions to use a certain amount of coercion in bargaining wage rates and work conditions.

However, in recent years the balance of power between capital and labour has been shifted very notably towards the former. At the same time direct taxation has been considerably lowered for the highest earners and only marginally for the average earner. Taken together the policies of the present government have produced a considerable widening of the gap between incomes across the population: unemployment has increased over a five-year period between 300 and 400%, statutory services have been cut back (always to the greater disadvantage of the already less well-off), and State benefits, which have not always been increased in line with inflation, are in some cases more difficult to receive. Meanwhile, the rights of unions to negotiate freely with employers have been considerably restricted.

Undeniably, the Government's policy changes are based on a fixed ideological view of which values should be allowed to predominate throughout society. At the top of the list comes a particular concept of freedom – the freedom of business to create wealth and expand in ways determined almost exclusively by economic power in the market. In theory, this value is justified on the basis that, in the long run, it will allow both the industrial and service sectors of the economy to have a secure base, and therefore to expand and create 'real' jobs. In practice, this kind of freedom, when not offset by other values, such as the strengthening of the local community and priority care for the most disadvantaged sectors of society, leads to an increasingly unfair distribution of income, ownership of wealth and opportunities for work. In other words, according to a Marxist view of economic power-structures in society, the values most championed at present are precisely the ones which guarantee that the present wealth-owners

27

consolidate their privileged position. It is a classic case of the operation of ideology. Those Christians who tend to agree with liberation theology believe that the ideology is unacceptable because it conflicts with the nature of God as portrayed in the Old and New Testaments.

The point of the ideological critique is to discern the hidden agendas and motives of people's legitimation of policies. Surely, from a theological point of view (sin as self-deception), one has to be suspicious of arguments and policies which leave the privileges of the rich and powerful intact and in practice continue to deprive the disadvantaged of those resources which would allow them to live dignified human lives? At the same time, I would also reject some of the main Marxist solutions to current social and economic problems, also on theological grounds, because they spring from a basically humanist, utopian world-view which is ultimately incompatible with the Christian understanding of redemption and the 'not yet' of the coming Kingdom.

This whole discussion gives a considerable number of perspectives from which a Christian community can reflect theologically. The claims and counter-claims concerning the causes of deprivation and impoverishment will need to be carefully weighed. In particular the local Church will need to ask itself what view of human beings predominates in both the Marxist account of conflict and the capitalist account of the harmony of interests. It might best understand the disparate views by engaging in discussion with both articulate local Marxists (there may be some, for example, among trade union leaders, community development workers, teachers, etc.) and defenders of the Government's view of economic realities (perhaps among members of a local chamber of commerce). To what extent is conflict endemic in the actual reality of human societies according to the Bible? How far does the Bible envisage the possibility of change towards greater equality and participation? By what means should that change come? For example, would it ever be right for citizens to go outside a parliamentary resolution of problems (i.e. by majority vote of elected political representatives) and be involved in civil disobedience in order to achieve the redressing of important grievances?[15]

Another series of questions has to do with the Church's role in aiding and abetting the continuance of a situation of privilege for some. To what extent does the message the Church proclaims, or, equally, fails to proclaim, tacitly support the consensus of those who dispose of power in the nation? How far do Christians believe that one of the purposes of faith is to cement society and bring stability to the nation? To what extent does the message of the gospel upset normal assumptions concerning rights in society (e.g. all the statements about the outsiders inheriting the Kingdom of God – Matt. 19.30; 20:16; Luke 13.30; 14.21–3; 16.25)?

The Church has a divine mandate to be engaged in a constant work of reconciliation: first and foremost challenging and inviting people to end their indifference towards God and find him to be their living Saviour through Jesus Christ; but also bringing people together wherever there is misunderstanding, dispute or conflict. However, the Church sometimes falls into the trap of substituting pacification for reconciliation, seeking to conciliate between two parties without taking a proper account of underlying issues of justice and truth.

A local community might like to reflect Christianly on local examples of conflict and consider ways in which it might possibly be an instrument of genuine reconciliation in the situation. It would need to look closely at Jesus' work of atonement as the supreme demonstration of what reconciliation really means – a way of ending a situation of hostility in which justice is satisfied and mercy and forgiveness are fully exercised, remembering that, from a biblical perspective, justice has a lot to do with championing the cause of people who carry no weight in the community.

The study of reconciliation as a task for the Church, using case studies from real life, would not be complete without taking into account cultural values and norms which are peculiarly English. No theological reflection today can ignore the central place of culture without being guilty of extreme naivety. Thus, in this case, a Christian community would need to come to grips with the almost unqualified distaste that the English have for 'extreme' solutions (for example, the general reaction to the miners' strike) and their desire to find, where possible, moderate, compromising (understand 'sensible') ways forward. In the light of the biblical revelation of God in Jesus Christ, is this cultural characteristic a correct intuition of the genuine path to a healing of relationships, or is it a papering-over of deep-seated discriminations which always has the effect of leaving the ruling classes in the ascendancy?

Liberation theology would tend to say that the way power operates in a capitalist economy is idolatrous, and Christians can never compromise with idolatry. To do so in this case is to buy into the tacit ideology of a culture which has passively allowed the acquisition of wealth to rule supreme over all other values. Is not the apparent ineffectiveness of the Church a simple confirmation of the fact that it believes that its adherence to middle-class values is more important than its faithfulness to the gospel?

CONCLUSION

The topics which need serious theological discussion from within Urban Priority Areas, if not endless, are nevertheless manifold. To end, we could mention another three.

First, there is the question of the quality of life. In situations of gross social negligence and indifference it is natural to focus on redressing a balance in such a way that deprived people have greater access to things which make for physical well-being. Liberation theology has often been accused of too materialist a view of poverty, and thus of falling into the trap of Western culture – of equating progress with the power to own. Though this is an unfair criticism, the poor, biblically speaking, are not simply those lacking the basic necessities of life. The Bible lays tremendous emphasis on interpersonal and community relationships. Where these are in disarray, particularly regarding the fundamental relationship with God, there is abject human poverty, or absence of *shalom*. Hence, poverty is a multidimensional reality. This truth must not be used to minimize the centrality of justice for the materially poor, but nor should poverty be so defined as to dehumanize those suffering physical deprivation. Poor communities can and do demonstrate a richness of human life which makes the daily existence of the rich look squalid and empty.

Second, there is the question of health. In a situation where each citizen can no longer expect necessarily to receive an unstinted attention from medical services, preventive medicine must surely become an increasing priority. Where even increased resources will not be able to match the growth in the expense of sophisticated medical techniques, society as a whole may have to make the hard and painful choice between different needs in health care, based on some kind of 'quality of life' criteria and on the special responsibility which the community has to respond to the needs of its most vulnerable members (for example, the handicapped). Health in the community is a deeply theological issue, for the Scriptures have much to say about what constitutes a healthy life. There is room for a good deal of reflection on the meaning of human wholeness, and in what ways the local Christian community can see part of its task as creating a greater awareness of the spiritual, moral and physical integrity of human beings in situations of deprivation.

Finally, there is the question of community development. The Church has a lot of experience to draw on from different parts of the world in the work of encouraging unempowered and vulnerable people to take responsibility for their own communities and, where necessary, to claim basic rights and resist oppression. The Church in English

Urban Priority Areas might well like to draw on this experience,[16] as it reflects on what enhances and what destroys communities, and the power of the gospel to transform despair, ugliness and inhumanity into hope, goodness and a new creation in Jesus Christ.

Notes

1 In an article entitled 'Theology for the Sake of Mission', to be published in *Anvil*.
2 cf. J. A. Kirk, *God's Word for a Complex World: Discovering How the Bible Speaks Today* (Marshall Pickering, 1987).
3 The Archbishop's Commission on Urban Priority Areas, *Faith in the City* (Church House Publishing, 1985), 3.36.
4 In his Introduction to the present volume.
5 ibid., p. 10.
6 cf. G. Gutierrez, 'Liberation Praxis and Christian Faith' in *The Power of the Poor in History* (SCM Press, 1983).
7 H. Assmann, 'Statement by Hugo Assmann' in S. Torres and J. Eagleson (eds), *Theology in the Americas* (New York, Orbis Books, 1976), p. 299.
8 For example, in the two Brandt Reports and at numerous UNCTAD meetings; cf. *World Development Crisis*, a 'Comment' pamphlet produced by The Catholic Institute for International Relations, August 1987.
9 C. Mesters, 'How the Bible is Interpreted in Some Basic Christian Communities' in H. Küng and J. Moltmann (eds), *Conflicting Ways of Interpreting the Bible* (T. & T. Clark, 1980), pp. 44 and 46.
10 cf. L. and C. Boff, *Introducing Liberation Theology* (Burns & Oates, 1987), p. 28.
11 L. Boff, *Teologia desde el Cautiverio* (Bogota, Indo-American Press Service, 1975), p. 32.
12 T. Hanks, *God So Loved the Third World* (New York, Orbis Books, 1983), p. 35.
13 cf. G. Cook, *The Expectation of the Poor* (New York, Orbis Books, 1985); L. Boff, *Ecclesiogenesis: The Basic Communities Reinvent the Church* (Collins, 1986).
14 *Faith in the City*, 3.29.
15 At the time of writing (March 1988) this is an issue related to the future of the National Health Service in the United Kingdom.
16 cf. C. Elliott, *Comfortable Compassion? Poverty, Power and the Church* (Hodder & Stoughton, 1987); M. Pennington (ed.), *A Handbook on World Development* (Shaftesbury Project, 1983), particularly section D – 'Case Studies'.

2
Images of the City and the Shaping of Humanity

Haddon Willmer

Faith in the City is a significant recent episode within the history of the Churches' concerns about the ways in which people live in modern urban society and what cities make of human beings. (I use the term 'city' as a shorthand or symbol for modern urban politically ordered society.) The long and continuing history of the city and the Churches is larger than *Faith in the City* and its sadly too exclusively Anglican outcomes. We are still living in the historical moment of *Faith in the City*, but it is on the way to becoming part of our remembered past, relativized by subsequent events. It is not yet obsolete, but in time its analysis and recommendations will be so. Because *Faith in the City* is a historical action, the concern of this essay is not to explain and vindicate the text of the Report but to reflect on the traditions of practice of which it is a part.

The Report could not have been made unless there were a broad living tradition of Christian practice preparing for it. The Report itself draws attention to this tradition;[1] but more revealing is the list of the places and people the Commissioners visited or consulted and the stories of the commissioners themselves. To take but one example: it is more than thirty years since David Sheppard went to the Mayflower Centre in London and thus engaged with the city in the tradition of the Settlements and Clubs founded in the late nineteenth century by men from the Universities of Oxford and Cambridge in poorer areas of London. Of course this form of Christian social involvement in what we now call Urban Priority Areas had all sorts of questionable characteristics, but it was better to risk paternalism and idealism than to pass by on the other side. Within a tradition of caring action and readiness to learn by living with people in the city, Sheppard was apprenticed. The Report represents and rests on such commitments; it relates to the practice of many Christians in various organizations and groups over many years.

It is not accidental that I speak more of the city than of Urban Priority Areas. The city has been 'a focus of civilization' since the middle of the fourth millennium BC.[2] In the city, 'man's esthetic and economic endeavors mesh . . . closely in corporeal form'. The city

32

has developed the 'sense of order out of which civilization grew and on which it depends'.[3] Cities are different from the mere extension of urbanization, of the kind which is alleged to be happening in the South-East of England as the pressure of population eats up the countryside. Such urban sprawl may indeed now be destroying the city in many places because its results are difficult to manage politically and they do not give a convincing visual manifestation of a working human order. Sprawl has no centre or shape.

In this respect, my emphasis is different from that of *Faith in the City*. Despite its title and its intentions signalled in a few paragraphs,[4] the Report is concerned above all with Urban Priority Areas, and its effect in some quarters has been to distinguish them from their total social context. In order to give Urban Priority Areas the priority they deserve, they must be seen within the 'city', the whole political setting in which and because of which they occur. The Report does not deny the importance of the political view, but for a variety of reasons it was not sufficiently developed. *Faith in the City* is rooted in the traditions of pragmatic social science, which provided the intellectual backbone of the post-1945 consensus. Urban Priority Areas are identified by multiple indicators of a statistical sort. They are territories which can be drawn on maps, with high 'Z' scores, and thus marked off for specific treatment. There is a danger that the impression is created that the problem of the Urban Priority Areas can be discerned and tackled in detachment from the dynamics of the whole society, with its economy and politics, provided – and this is a challenging proviso – enough resources are devoted to them. The truth lies in the other direction. The existence of Urban Priority Areas reveals something about the working of the whole economic, political and moral system in which we all live. Urban Priority Areas demand direct and immediate action; they also drive inquiry back to the city.

The city is corporate human power in positive self-assertion and activity. It is both the framework within which problems occur and that within which they may be tackled. The city symbolizes the way people live together so that they are able to achieve significant control over their own humanity. The city thus incorporates some view of humanity in its workings. It is at any time a statement about the bounds and possibilities of human beings. The city is the working answer given to questions like: What kind of goodness can human beings realize? Are human beings one community or many? What is the relation between kindness and kinship? How near to genuine equality and freedom can we come? Such questions arouse others: May we realistically read the city as a meaningful moral concretization of responsible humanity? Is the good and well-doing city (political community) possible? These questions require us to confront our pessimism again and again. Perhaps the city fails to open up a good human possibility. It may rather show we are caught in a level of human helplessness and structured incompetence broader than what is painfully evident in the Urban Priority Areas.

We concentrate on the city to ask what cities make of human beings. What sort of humanity is encouraged and enabled by different sorts of city? Human well-being is our criterion for reflection on the quality of the social order within which people live. How is human well-being to be assessed? The general quality of life can be represented by statistics of the total money-measured wealth of the country, of how it is growing and how it is shared. To these statistics other measures (such as those of literacy, health and crime) could be added. Such statistics would allow us to make some broad judgements about what chances people have of being healthy and happy human beings, but it is well not to put great faith in them. The criteria of human well-being need to be worked out also in terms of the value of persons and the significance of personal experiences. Such criteria make political management much harder, if not impossible, but politics needs to be open to realities it cannot manage. It is right to insist, with William Temple, on the priority of persons as made in the image of God: so 'the State exists for its citizens, not citizens for the State' (or any other political organization or collective).⁵ In dealing with questions of the distribution of wealth and poverty in our society it is good practice to listen to individuals, for it is in people that we can see what is happening to humanity in the city.⁶ Of course we have to go on trying to manage our living together within the limits of our political skills, but we need to be continually and genuinely disturbed by meeting living evidence of the inability of human beings living and working together as the city to do adequate justice to the needs, potential, sensitivity and worth of all human beings as persons. It is good that Members of Parliament hold 'surgeries' so long as they, the MPs, are really cut up by them and do not use them to cut down or out those who consult them.

What the city makes of human beings cannot be read off safely from general statistics. It is not, however, a question to be ducked by pleading the immeasurable variety of human beings as persons, which is beyond our capacity to grasp. In order to advance on this issue where we may not retreat, we have to make use of other measures too. One such measure would be a consideration of the type of person represented by the ideals and morality of the city. What role models are on offer in the city? What styles of human living are made easier by being materially supported and applauded? By the articulation of ideals, people are enabled, though not coerced, to see themselves in certain ways and to develop in certain directions, while other ways are discouraged. To know what the city is making of humanity is thus as much a matter for cultural, religious and historical study as it is for economic statistics. We are not here looking merely at what the moral teachers in a city say, but at what the city says to people about their humanity through its institutions, policies and actions. What people are told they ought to do is not always the same as what the city enables or encourages them to do.

PROPHECY

Probably we ought not to be totally pessimistic about the possibility of the city's shaping people's humanity for good through what it actually does. There is, however, no city without the need for prophets, who, for the sake of humanity, teach ideals and morality which are in tension with what the city is actually making of humanity. In Britain today we cannot do without prophecy, which is why the Churches should not be intimidated by the tension between them and the State. Of itself, that tension does not prove they are being prophetic; they might just be trouble-makers; but if there is no tension, they can be certain they are not verging on the prophetic. Beyond the question of whether or not the Church is prophetic is the issue of the variety of ways the possibly prophetic can relate to the institutionalized working order of the city. In a concentration camp, prophecy is impossible: there can only be protest and subversion. That is because the dynamics of the camp, by which it is what it is, give prophecy no opportunity. Prophecy cannot speak to people in the camp to call them back to the basic good values of the form of society they live in: there is nothing to appeal to. Morality and humanity are in simple opposition to the camp and are given no foothold by it. Is Britain today to be understood in a similar way? It is alarming that there are those who think that all we can do is protest and be separate and work for a radically different order. Such a judgement needs to be considered carefully. Many of the Churches' discussions are confused because of the divide between those who take this view and others who think that prophecy is possible since there is still much in our society and its ordering that can be appealed to and built on.

There may be another level of complication that needs to be taken into account in any discussion of prophecy in Britain today. There are different schools of prophecy, recalling people to different views of our British past and to different forms of society partially present in our traditions. All prophets relate positively to what they are in critical tension with. But because they are prophets and not totally alienated protesters they are enculturated in some part of our society, with its values and traditions. To be enculturated in one part is likely to mean being ignorant and unappreciative of some other part. Therefore prophecy involves conflict among the prophets as well as between them and society. What prophecy we have may therefore sound very like political debate. That should not be used to invalidate or silence the prophets, but it requires us to develop an ear for the prophetic word being spoken in ordinary political debates. What enables prophets is in the last resort not only what the prophets say, but that others, even a city, have an ear that can pick up the message. Without that ear, prophets would become unprophetic alienated protesters. What ear is there in Britain? How do we hear? What forms our hearing? Does the city shape us so that we cannot hear? Are we being deafened to that most prophetic of voices, the cry of the poor?

We tend to think of prophecy as though it were the activity of a special class of insightful and perhaps inciting persons, set over against society and the average run of people. Some may think the Quakers go too far in believing that there is that of God in every one, but their views helps us to understand prophecy better. For the public prophet will not be heard unless there is prophetic receptivity in people. By virtue of their receptivity and capacity to listen, many people are prophets or have a prophetic side to them. If that is so, we should expect to meet the prophet not simply in some other person, who bears down upon us with his 'Thus saith the Lord' and other appropriate signs, but in ourselves. And this prophetic side of our being gives us the ear for the prophets outside ourselves. If we have this ear because the city has so formed us, it is evidence that there is something good about the city; there is something in the city to which we can relate prophetically rather than as alienated protesters and denouncers of doom.

What can the prophet appeal to? What ideals or values are in any way operative in the city, inherent in its workings or manifest in its symbols? That is far too large a question to be answered in a short essay; values can be investigated in so many ways, some of them very detailed and scientific. Here I want to draw attention to some ways in which the city in Britain has been informed by images derived from cities known to us historically like Jerusalem and Athens. These cities have served as images of the ideal city, which might inspire us in our attempts at city-building. They are prophetic, or aids to prophecy, not merely because they set an ideal before us, but because they interpret our own political experience to us, giving us patterns within which we can see shape in the multifarious and confusing incidents and encounters that make up our living together. These images do not merely help us to make sense of what is, they also invite us to dream and to work for a better city. These images are prophetic because they are two-sided: they connect both with what is, discovering what is going on, and with what is yet to be, inviting us towards its potential or promise. If they do not manage to make that connection between what is and what is to come, these images cannot be prophetic. They will fall on one side or the other of the polarization (which is the death of prophecy) between complacent or despairing conservatism, which holds on to what it has because there can be nothing better, and alienated protest and abdication, which seeks another world having no connection with where we are. Are these images still prophetic for us?

JERUSALEM

Jerusalem is a religious symbol of the city, open to various interpretations in, and after, the Bible. In much of the Christian tradition, following Augustine, Jerusalem has become heavenly and lies in the future for those who are its citizens. On earth they are strangers and pilgrims with no abiding city. Others have taken Jerusalem as a model and a task for our political activity. In the Psalms, Jerusalem is celebrated as the city where the people gather together to worship God. God is to be worshipped for his mighty deeds, some of which are monumentalized in Jerusalem itself (Ps. 48.12-14). Is is God who defends the city: 'Unless the Lord watches over the city, the watchman stays awake in vain' (Ps. 127.1). God gives his peace to the city and requires those who live in it to share his peace with one another. Hence, the city is called to realize a justice which is more than giving each person his due: it is to give God his due, by building the city that his peace, presence and forgiveness make possible, so that all his people may share it together. Jerusalem is where the tribes go up and where together they find what has the ultimate claim upon them, 'above my highest joy' (Ps. 137.6). It is the city where there is nothing to make people grieve or feel afraid or go hungry or feel despised and neglected (Rev. 21—22).

One obstacle to our working with this image of the city is that it is inextricably theistic: the city is God's work as well as his place. Can this mean anything for our largely secularized politics? We are not the first people to face this question: the history of biblical Jerusalem was a sobering secularizing experience. Jerusalem was seen as the city of God only by faith which reached beyond the fragmentary hints evident in its actual life. Can such faith express itself only by looking beyond this world to a Jerusalem kept in heaven? Or is the city we seek by faith one which can have genuine though never complete realization in our work of building and running the earthly city? Whether or not it wins our theological approval, the image of the 'national Jerusalem', as David Deans called it in Sir Walter Scott's *The Heart of Midlothian*, has focused the prayers and political participation of many people in modern Britain. Its most famous expression has been William Blake's 'Jerusalem'.

This vision of Jerusalem was massively denied by life in modern industrial towns and cities. In the nineteenth century many people realized that a human quality of life was not possible in them. Human beings died young from many avoidable causes. Too many of those who survived had to struggle with adverse conditions so that their health was damaged, their spirits broken, their educational development stunted, their sociality warped. The cities needed to be changed to enable a more truly human kind of person and community.

Action was taken on the basis that the full humanity of people could be enabled by the physical shaping of the city and the provision of decent housing and various public facilities. G. M. Trevelyan said Robert Owen first clearly taught the 'modern doctrine' that 'environment makes character and that environment is under human control'.[7] Communities – or groups acting at least professedly on behalf of communities, though not without some obvious or subtle elements of self-interest – set about improving cities and even inventing new kinds of cities. In the twentieth century, planning became more comprehensive; even without the Second World War, which cleared the ground, our towns and cities would have been bulldozed and rebuilt, thanks to the enthusiasm of planners. Urban redevelopment has been conditioned by many practical constraints and financial interests but it has not lacked vision which gave it some hope of eventual coherence. It is not surprising, therefore, to find the story of modern British town planning told in terms of the quest to build the New Jerusalem.[8] *Faith in the City* was written in this tradition at a time when it was already falling into disarray and was widely as well as wilfully discredited.

Attempting to build Jerusalem in England's green and pleasant land, in the belief that environment enables humanity, is now criticized for creating dependency in people. It is said it takes away their independence and will to work and be responsible for themselves. Social engineering, as it is sometimes called, is therefore a cause of many of our troubles. The quest for the heavenly Jerusalem as the other-worldly haven from all the struggles of this life has often been accused of sapping the will for this world's work. Now it is alleged the same pattern repeats itself where the expectation of a new earthly Jerusalem – or the assumption that we have a right to it or that we can enjoy it even while it is half-built and half-paid for – makes people unwilling or unable to work and suffer realistically. While there is much to be said for such criticism of the New Jerusalem tradition, it is first necessary to appreciate its positive truth.

It does not necessarily imply a deterministic view that circumstances produce human beings. There is no need to think in those terms to see the necessity of changing urban conditions. Let us accept that what people are has roots in spontaneous desires and efforts which are beyond precise political management and cannot be directly or totally determined by outward material circumstances, as a die shapes metal. It is still the case that what people can desire depends on what they think is open to them and on the energy they have to work for it. Those who are poor and have no helper will see, unless they are stupid, that very little is open to them and will attempt little. Those who have to spend most of their energy getting barely enough, maybe not enough, of the basic necessities of life, will not have energy to make more of themselves. Those who have frequently suffered disappointments in the struggles with poverty, and who find they are kept at the bottom, in poverty amidst plenty, ought not to be condemned as lazy or cowardly or unenterprising if they give up the struggle. Certainly those who have never known the discouragements of living with inadequate material resources have no right either to criticize such people or to order society so that they are left without generous help, in the naive hope, derived from a one-sided knowledge of human nature, that putting such people under further pressure will do them good.

I am ashamed that words like these need to be written in Britain in 1989, as though we had forgotten lessons our Victorian forebears learnt at great cost. Those who say that people's capacity to be hopeful, reliable and enterprising is independent of their material conditions or those who argue from this assertion to justify doing little to improve those conditions are rarely living with low and precarious incomes themselves, in bad housing, in poor health, and with low social status. The loudest preachers of the possibility of being good in bad conditions are rarely speaking from the test of experience. Nor are they speaking within the fellowship of the city, which is a political community that includes both the exhorters and their audience; they rather shout across the alienations and inequalities that divide our society and are physically evident in the existence of Urban Priority Areas, those parts of cities which have for too long been at the end of the queue.

This political argument recalls fundamental theological issues about the nature of human freedom and dependency. The Christian tradition has wrestled with this question throughout its history.

Human beings are created by God; they are creatures who have been given otherness from God; they are not extended parts of God's own being, nor are they inert in his hands. They are radically free, not merely from other beings but from their Creator. Yet this freedom is finite because it is given freedom: whatever other limits it may have, its decisive limit is that it is given by God. It is not to be counted as a possession owned despite God, let alone to be seized by an act of robbery from him. God-given freedom is not inhuman; it is the freedom to be human. It serves the nature and purpose of human beings who are made for God and find fulfilment in relation with God. Being made for God does not mean that humanity is dissolved into God; it means finding and using the given freedom to be human in God's way for humanity, a freedom disclosed in humanity itself, significantly in God-become-human in Jesus with the ordinary humanity of one who comes 'eating and drinking'. Humanity is a gift of God and implies continual openness to God's giving. The gift of God, our true humanity, is not a gift given once for all; it is like manna in the wilderness, given to us a day at a time. Our human being is always then a mixture of dependence and freedom; a dependent freedom, which is not felt as a constriction but as a liberation. Theologically, therefore, it is not necessary to set dependency and freedom over against each other.

How does God give us the freedom to be human as he intends? Does God give this freedom to us in our life in the city or is it only available in some spiritual realm which human beings as political animals cannot inhabit? God has apparently not created us for the freedom of disembodied, asocial angels who are his direct agents. God makes bodily social creatures to bear his image. He sets them in families and peoples. In doing so, God ensures that his gift of freedom would have to come to human beings through the mediation of humanity. Human dependencies are not necessarily bondage and oppression. They may be the dependencies in which we find ourselves freed to be human. God does not make us directly dependent on himself, so that the freedom we thereby are given is purely spiritual and unable either to illumine or to be realized in the life of the city. God gives us life within networks of natural and human dependencies which he does not destroy but rather respects because they are intrinsic to his creative concept. He plays consistently within the rules of his own game. It is obvious that human dependencies do not serve the liberating purpose of God with complete faithfulness; but God is faithful to his creation and continually works to keep it open and serviceable to his purpose. This God may be seen in Jesus Christ. God becomes human out of respect for, and faithfulness to, the integrity of his gift to human beings in creating them human. For Christians, it is through Jesus Christ, God-made-man, that our radical dependence on God is established. In Jesus Christ, God lives a human freedom which is dependent. This humanity is not purely dependent on God; it risks and endures and redeems dependence on other human beings. Jesus is handed over to men, and is dependent on them for what becomes of him and his cause. The giving of the Holy Spirit, the outcome of the whole life and sacrifice of Jesus, does not cancel the truth that God gives freedom to human beings in and through their living of human life together, so that freedom comes out of our dependence on others. For the Holy Spirit is not a sign that God has changed his method and, having tried to work through humanity in Jesus, now turns to a direct spiritual communication with individuals who can thus claim to be in touch with God without any dependence on other human beings. If that were so, of course, we could claim that we can be truly and properly dependent on God even while treating human beings as independent of each other. No, the Holy Spirit means that God is still pursuing his way with human beings through human beings. The way he worked in Jesus, choosing humanity as the means of the full revelation of God, is being universalized through the Spirit. He acts everywhere and in everything by the Spirit, who remains hidden but moves people to build and act in community (Gal. 5.13—6.5; Rom. 8.22-27; 12.1-21) and to be Christ to one another.

Humanity and embodiment are social: so the grace of God is humanly mediated by multiple channels. The surrounding grace of God makes human beings the objects of God's love and establishes them as of inestimable value to God and so of course for themselves and each other. God's grace operates through many channels, to make this truth real to people. God wants his love to get through to people effectively to bring them to the full humanity he intends for them. His love does not disdain any means, certainly not any means inherent in the creation God made. Every part of humanity may be used by God as a channel of his grace to people, for he works through every created agency and avenue that he finds open or can open. So there is no theological reason why material conditions and the conduct of governments and economies and cities should not be used by God. That puts on all, including governments, the obligation to make themselves available to God for his work and not to escape into some spiritual but unchristian delegation of participating in his affairs to the Churches and other minority agencies. 'The means of grace' – anything which gives 'hope of glory' – includes potentially the social system, or the city. If we do not there find dependencies that liberate, we shall find dependencies that oppress; and the worst kind of oppressions are created by those who refuse to acknowledge dependency, who lust after independence, like Lucifer, and who therefore do not know how dependent they are on God through others and do not work to liberate those who are dependent on them.

At present in our society the responsibility of individuals is being preached with vehemence. To order society successfully, more trust is placed in the demands of the law than in generous grace. There are, however, hints that even the strongest advocates of individualism know something in practice of the gracious reality of society which is denied in theory. The family is said to be very important. It is a place of refuge and support; people need such a place for dependency; there is no better start in life than to have the gifts of a good family and education. Now, the family shows that individuals are not responsible out of total self-sufficiency. If the family is so important to the maintenance of efficient human beings, should we not move forward with the same logic and perception of human nature to interpret what lies beyond the limits of family? The family which does this job is fragile: it needs to be located in supportive political community. The family is not universally available. If individuals need such families, what about those who do not have families? Do they not need to be living in the kind of society which will encompass them with familial care? If families can and should care for people, so that people can depend upon them and be equipped to live responsibly, why cannot other institutions and groups work in the same way, both towards individuals and towards families? The preaching of the family by politicians will be empty and unhelpful if what some learn about the grace of life in a good family – that it is social – is not the basis on which we attempt to build the whole city, the total political community in which we live, which in the end is the global human family. The dangers of dependency are being dangerously exaggerated by one-sided analysis. As a result, we are not enjoying the blessings of well-ordered mutual and liberating dependencies in our society.

ATHENS

It is unhistorical and unfair to suppose that the dangers of dehumanizing dependency were not recognized by many who believed that human beings needed the grace of a good environment. William Temple, for example, argued that 'society must be so arranged as to give to every citizen the maximum opportunity for making deliberate choices and the best possible training for the use of that opportunity'.[9] Images derived from the city-state of Athens helped to restrain any tendency to feather-bedded dependency lurking in the New Jerusalem model. Athens celebrated citizenship as active participation in the affairs of the political community. As the franchise was progressively extended to all adults in Britain this vision of citizenship gained plausibility. As in Athens, however, citizenship involved more than voting, of which they had much more in Athens anyway. There had to be intelligible debate, directed to the public and not confined to a narrow political circle. This kind of public life could be promoted in some measure by advancing education and by serviceable media. Also necessary was experience of participation in political life and action. In that respect, little Athens, with its direct democracy and its slaves, was not a model that could ever be fully realized in Britain. It was, nevertheless, an image which inspired aspects of our politics. Some entered the vision of participatory politics through the trade unions. War or the threat of war broke up the mental or geographical seclusion in which many lived, forcing them to think as citizens.[10] The Labour victory of 1945 was significantly helped by the political education many acquired, formally and informally, in the armed forces. Others discovered being citizens as a significant dimension of their being human through participating in local politics.

Modern British local government developed in the hope that, through it, citizenship would become real for more people. The hope had some plausibility at least for a few people in a few generations. Its plausibility was aided by the education many people were given: they heard about Athens, and even about the medieval guilds. If they could not precisely re-enact contemporary equivalents, they could interpret the very different modern experience of politics in terms of these visions.

Today, does it not have to be admitted that this vision and the drive to realize it has broken down? Education no longer sustains it. The reform of local government in 1974 swept away much of the symbolism of local patriotisms. The dominant value behind the reform was efficiency of administration rather than participation in local, historically developed communities with meaningful identities. These changes cannot, however, be blamed purely on the insensitivity of centralizing government. There were many reasons why the tradition of local government had not realized the idealistic quest for citizenship as real humanizing participation in corporate self-governing life together. The ideal, even the make-believe, expressed in terms of imagery derived from Athenian or other experiences, could not endlessly overcome and be imposed on our own situation, which is not local but mobile. The motor car rather than the city is its image and its power.

For all its pain, and the immense dangers of dehumanizing cultural impoverishment through the loss of the past, our present situation has the merit that it invites us to live our own lives and to take responsibility for them rather than to exist vicariously, borrowing parts to play from the repertoire of the long and rich histories in which we know ourselves to stand. To know that our political life is not Athenian and should not be squeezed into that image might be an element of gain in what many feel to be a loss. In any case we have to make the best of it. The truth of our situation is not, however, that we have replaced historically derived ideals with some better, workable and human ideal. We delude ourselves if we suppose that is the case. In our politics now, we are more nakedly open to the basic human question: What shall our humanity be?

A NEW IMAGE

What indeed is our humanity now, in so far as it is shaped by our life together in political community? It is not defined for us by Athens or Jerusalem, however suggestive such images continue to be for many of us. It might be well to face the gloomy possibility that we are invited to see ourselves by the city we live in as consumers. No longer is the city symbolized by the Town Hall where a political community deliberates about its well-being and development; the city's symbol is the shopping centre where people can find what they want. Perhaps from this vantage-point the truth is discovered about older forms of citizenship: even old town politics was like a market for those who could get into it. People went into politics for what they could get out of it. The political ideal collapses in the face of the cynic's recognition that we are all consumers; the only differences are that people have different tastes and buying power. Many of the messages that come to them are invitations to consume; many of their forays into society are as consumers. We not only consume food and drink and goods from shops. We consume education and health-care, which are understood as businesses directed towards giving the customer what he wants. We consume the world as tourists. As impotent spectators of 'news', we consume the history and sufferings of others.

Some do not have the resources to be consumers; to be poor is to be forced to know oneself as a consumer, ever struggling to satisfy basic needs and never getting free from them. This is the dependence of the poor. Affluence, the freedom to consume without worry about paying, is equally a form of dependence. Our social order is such that many can assume a large measure of power to consume, while others merely dream of it. Affluence allows us to be consumers and as such we are dependent on the way the social order works. The affluent protect themselves from disasters within the social order; but a disaster to the social order would take away what they depend on. While it holds, the affluent can take the social order for granted; they can be apolitical. And the affluent live such busy lives, consuming things and people, that they sustain the illusion that they are actively and even creatively living their own lives. Their dependence on all they consume is hidden from them; they despise dependence and those who are obviously dependent; they cannot build a society of grace. If the affluent consumer has any inkling of what the world is like, he gets locked into a fearful protectiveness of what he has. That reveals his basic dependence.

The affluent lacks public spirit, not so much because he is selfish, but because the city offers no possibility save that of being a consumer, a passive and anxious dependant.

Of course, human beings have it in them to be more than consumers, affluent or poor. They want to be more. And the city requires more. At the least, it needs producers. Hence it must develop ways to get people to work harder and produce more, but the best ways it knows confirm people's view of themselves as consumers: 'If a man will not work, let him not eat.' 'In order to be a consumer, you must produce.' 'In order to do well for your family, you must get on.' It is implied in exhortations of this sort that if people did not know themselves to be consumers, with escalating demands, there would be no adequate means of motivating them to work or of disciplining them. People as voters behave as irresponsible consumers of public services, supporting policies without regard for what they cost. Privatization and the poll-tax are both attempts to control the situation by treating people as consumers. The national and local political communities are reduced to supermarkets of services for sale; everything has its price for those who can pay. The life of political community is no longer a celebration of our humanity which transcends our being consumers. The city offers us no other common definition of our humanity.

Is this the end of our road? Do we have to submit to the city's definition of us as consumers, especially since its power over us derives from the basic needs of our existence? Are those who have a fuller vision of what it is to be human doomed to make unavailing protests against the city they cannot effectively subvert? Or is there some hope for prophecy here? Can the city of consumers be the place where we learn afresh what it is to be human in God's way or does consumerism inflict upon us a necessary irremediable blindness? Through the inadequate and masked forms of dependence we know as consumers, can we learn what it is to live by grace? In the distorted freedom necessary to a consumer society, can we find the freedom to develop communities of resistance, endurance, and innovation? May the experience of responsibility that comes to us as consumers lead us to take responsibility for our common humanity, which is most crucially seen in the question of the humanity, not of myself, but of those I am most likely to overlook? Whether we respond to these questions as subversive protesters against an irredeemable society or as prophets who bring out what is good and hopeful in society against its own betrayals of its promise, to ask these questions will release us from seeing humanity merely as it is being defined by the city these days. We will at least imagine – and then we may be able to work for – a city which enables a citizenship which is something more than the right to consume. And the closer prophecy is driven to being simple protest against society, the more the religious element will be significant; in our struggle, we may look to God with deeper faith, hope and love, because there humanity is faithfully kept for us, over against any city which robs us of humanity or seduces us into surrendering it for a 'single meal' (Heb. 12.16).[11] The images of Athens and Jerusalem cannot be models for us in any simple way, but they may haunt the edges of our vision as useful reminders and witnesses of our human calling in the city.

Notes

1 The Archbishop's Commission on Urban Priority Areas, *Faith in the City* (Church House Publishing, 1985), ch. 3.
2 C. Tunnard, 'The Customary and the Characteristic: A Note on the Pursuit of City Planning History' in O. Handlin and J. Burchard (eds), *The Historian and the City* (The Joint Center for Urban Studies of the Massachusetts Institute of Technology and Harvard University, 1963), p. 217.
3 S. L. Thrupp, 'The City as the Idea of Social Order', ibid., p. 122.
4 *Faith in the City*, 1.47; 1.50; 3.29.
5 W. Temple, *Christianity and the Social Order* (1942; new edn SPCK, 1976), p. 40.
6 cf. D. B. Forrester and D. Skene, *Just Sharing* (Epworth, 1988), ch. 1; R. Banks, *All the Business of Life* (Albatross Books, 1987).
7 G. M. Trevelyan, *English Social History* (Longman, 1942), p. 484.
8 J. Stevenson, 'The New Jerusalem' in L. M. Smith, *The Making of Britain: Echoes of Greatness* (Macmillan, 1988), pp. 53–70.
9 Temple, *Christianity and the Social Order*, p. 44.
10 R. Hillary, *The Last Enemy* (Macmillan, 1942); A. Koestler, *Arrival and Departure* (Cape, 1943); P. Addison, *The Road to 1945* (Cape, 1975).
11 D. Soelle, *Christ the Representative* (SCM Press, 1967).

3
Theological Reflections on 'Community'

Andrew Hake

Faith in the City laid considerable emphasis on 'community', and claimed that the Christian religion has a contribution to make to the theory and practice of community work based both on its experience of *koinonia* and its theology of God, humankind and the Church: 'this Christian pattern of personal relationships within a community authorises the Church both to support and to challenge the principles which govern community work in Britain today'.[1] This is a bold claim, and demands further substantiation.

Attempts to bring theology to bear on community are hindered by the difficulty of reaching a working definition. Community is an aerosol word, popularly sprayed into discussions, giving a sweet scent and a hint of mist, clouding analysis. It is notorious that there is a mass of competing definitions. But all exist within the general framework of a discussion of personal relationships between human beings in groups, in society, and in the total 'human community'. Within this framework the Bible and the Christian tradition have much to say that is relevant to our present situation. I shall arrange my suggestions under four headings: *Covenant, Communication and the Common Language, Conflict* and *Communion*.

COVENANT

A covenant community

Although, as we shall see, the Bible is primarily concerned with particular 'communities' – Israel in the Old Testament, the Church in the New – it also provides a secure basis for the conviction that there is a wider community, embracing the whole of humanity, in which every human being has equivalent rights, accountability and dignity.

This perception does not belong to the oldest strata in the Old Testament. But after the Exile, when the Jews had been in forced contact with the cultures of the Mesopotamian world (including Babylonian creation myths), the priestly college re-edited the Hexateuch, weaving the 'P' stratum into the history. Elaborating on

47

the earlier (J) tradition, they set the story of Israel's special covenant relationship with Yahweh in the context of the whole creation. Yahweh was the originating personal power who had created humankind (male and female) 'in his own image'. Although this phrase is not explained, it is clear that Yahweh is in a sense beyond gender, and that power over the earth is being delegated to humans to exercise lordship (in terms of domination) over the created order. Until recently, this has been taken to authorize the more or less ruthless technological exploitation of natural resources and the institutionalized domination of the strong over the weak. Today, we have come to see that this lordship must be exercised in responsible stewardship, not only for the created world, but for the entire human community. Cain's ironical question, 'Am I my brother's keeper?' has been decisively answered by Jesus' demonstration that anyone who shows compassion or excites our compassion is our neighbour, to whom we must show love and responsibility just as much as to a member of our own smaller 'community'.

The stories in the early part of Genesis are part of the 'primeval history' of the Old Testament. They provide several accounts of how the initial relationships of divine creation and blessing were broken. 'The whole world had become corrupted.' But another lesson is conveyed in the story of the Flood. God's judgement always ends with the promise of mercy; a new covenant was established by God, 'between me and you and every living creature that is with you, for all future generations'. The rainbow was given as the sign. This Noachic covenant is of the greatest importance, as it affirms Israel's faith in a basic relationship with God as Creator and Preserver of the entire created order and the whole of humankind. This is the foundation covenant seen as quite fundamental to human existence from the very outset of the divine project, and therefore projected back by the post-exilic writers on to the very first generations before the covenants with Abraham or with Moses (Gen. 9.1-17). God's concern for and presence with the entire 'human community' had come to be seen as more fundamental even than his covenant with a particular people. In the subsequent development of Judaism, these 'Noachic commandments' symbolized the belief that God placed the same basic moral demands upon all his human creatures.

This conviction that God is the God of all human beings, who therefore have value in his sight and are accountable to him, was of course shared by pagan philosophers in the time of Christ, at least to the point of recognizing certain common features of our moral and religious nature. But some races, or peoples, were still regarded as superior, and other categories (such as slaves) were denied rights altogether. A decisive advance is to be found in the New Testament. It was admittedly in the context of the breaking down of racial barriers between Jew and Gentile that Paul proclaimed his radical conviction that in Christ 'there is neither Jew nor Greek, there is neither slave nor free, there is neither male nor female' (Gal. 3.28). But this conviction rested not merely on the experience of a new human solidarity in Christ which transcended all human distinctions, but on an understanding of what it is to be human in a world where Jesus Christ is Lord of all and is 'designated by God as judge of the living and the dead' (Acts 10.42, NEB). As Peter is reported to have said in the house of Cornelius:

> I now see how true it is that God has no favourites, but that in every nation the man who is godfearing and does what is right is acceptable to him. He sent his word to the Israelites and gave the good news of peace through Jesus Christ, who is Lord of all (Acts 10.34–36, NEB).

In Paul's words, the secret purpose of God, now revealed in Christ, was 'to unite all things in him, things in heaven and things on earth' (Eph. 1.10). From this perception grew the principle, which had never been fully accepted by ancient philosphers, that every member of the human community without exception is of value to God and has worth and dignity in his sight. Upon this rests the comparatively modern consensus that every human being, simply by virtue of being human, has certain inalienable rights which all states and governments have a responsibility to respect and promote. The world-wide protection sought for 'human rights' today testifies to a general recognition that there is a community that embraces all human beings.

Within this world-wide community there are of course countless smaller communities of a national, ethnic or local kind, and it is with one such community that the Old Testament is primarily concerned. The Old Testament may be seen as comprising the stories of a 'laboratory experiment' in community living. For many primal peoples, myths of origin, of common descent, are a basic element in the ethnic identity of a community. Such myths are powerful constellations of stories, often mingling strands of history, legend, interpretation, poetry, ideas and propaganda. Their effectiveness does not depend on their historical 'truth', but on the extent to which the myth accords with experienced reality. Whatever the exact history of the collection of nomadic Semitic tribes who occupied Canaan in the second millennium BC and formed a 'sacral alliance' there, their subsequent stories point to a tradition that they originated from a common stock linked by blood-ties.

The whole of the sacred Jewish Scriptures, however, witness to a decisive experience which transcends the myth of common origin, distinguishing the children of Israel from the cultures of the neighbouring peoples of Canaan. The Book of Deuteronomy expresses and consolidates the victory (no doubt after processes of absorption and rejection) of the worshippers of Yahweh over the fertility-prosperity religion of the Canaanites. Israel's identity was affirmed as based not primarily on a relationship to the land, to their ancestors, to their kin, to their national successes, nor to a deity who controlled fertility (though at times it was all these), but to their God who was active in the stream of events we call history, who had revealed himself as their God and called them into a covenant.

Although this people commonly identified themselves as 'children of Abraham', the tradition of common descent from Abraham did not of itself constitute the community. Some descendants of Abraham were not within the community (such as the children of Ishmael – Gen. 21.11–21); others who were not descended from him could be included so long as they accepted circumcision, which was regarded as the essential sign of the covenant for all males. The special identity of Israel depended on an element of commitment that was required of each generation. God had chosen Israel as 'a people holy to the Lord your God'. This 'holiness' involved a total repudiation of all idolatrous attachments to other gods, and was expressed in three demands covering the entire life of the community: right-dealing, ritual cleanness and ethnic purity.

This last requirement marks the point where 'community' overlaps with race and nationhood. The holiness of Israel was understood as requiring that the nation must be preserved from biological dilution. The demands of the covenant for right-dealing and for cultic purity were binding only upon members of the holy community (including individual strangers and sojourners within its orbit). In this context, ethnic identity was strongly affirmed. Nation, tribe, clan and family all had an essential role in the divine scheme of things. Without them, individual life was inconceivable. The assertion of identity as the holy people of the covenant was felt to require a rigid cultural and ethnic purity. This legacy of the Old Testament, established when the Israelites were struggling for their special identity *vis-à-vis* neighbouring peoples in Canaan, was later reinforced in the post-exilic experiences of the Jewish people.

This militant nationalism was perhaps a necessary apprenticeship, disciplining the nation in national identity. In particular they had to be separate from others whose idolatry might lure them to betray the covenant relationship. This exclusive consciousness may be interpreted as in some senses the equivalent of an 'adolescent' stage of self-assertion over against the rest of the world. Nevertheless, such consciousness was tempered by the ultimate vision, as in the later Isaiah, of Israel trail-blazing, piloting the blessing in store for all peoples, a light to all nations. Alongside an exclusive concern for ethnic purity there was the vision that God would 'come to gather all nations and races, and they shall come and see my glory' (Isa. 66.18, NEB).

This tension between an exclusive national identity and a wider and more inclusive vocation reappears again and again in the history of the Church. The terms of the debate are of course changed. The new Israel is not a national, racial or even cultural entity. It is open to all, and has a universal vocation. At the same time it has to attend to and cherish its own identity, maintaining its doctrine and setting standards for behaviour, such that some individuals may have to be excluded because of their failure to conform. Like the old, the new Israel is a covenant people maintaining its identity by responding to the demands for holiness, purity of living and right belief, but responding also to its vocation to be accessible to all human beings and a force for good in all parts of the world. In this sense, the 'community' to which both Old and New Testaments bear witness offers a paradigm which is relevant to the problems of race, ethnic identity and pluralism in British society today.

Identity, pluralism and the common life

Ethnic or tribal identity (the 'we' of 'people like us') is a basic ingredient of human society. Ethnicity includes not only elements of common biological ('racial') characteristics, but a common culture, shared traditions and identity. It is a necessary starting-point for personal individual/corporate identity. In a wide sense, 'tribalism' is as characteristic of white society in Britain (and elsewhere) as it is of black or Asian minorities. As David Jenkins has pointed out, however, there is a terrible destructive potential in the affirmation of sectional corporate identities: *'That by which we identify ourselves and have our sense of identity, significance and belonging is also that by which we dehumanise others.'*[2]

We have noted that for Israel, at a certain stage of national development, there was a very strong affirmation of corporate ethnic (national and tribal) identity. The heart of the matter was neither common descent nor territoriality nor a common culture, but the shared conviction of a call into a covenant relationship with God. We have suggested that this was a necessary 'adolescent' stage of development, but, as with all human identities, there was, as we have seen, a deep ambiguity in this ethnic consciousness: Israel's special

51

experience as giving a right to privilege and superiority, or as opening the way to fulfilment for all humankind.

Jesus had clearly affirmed a Jewish superiority to the Syro-Phoenician woman (Matt. 15.26); but his compassion and sense of justice had forced him to stretch beyond the confines of his ethnic and cultural inheritance. On a number of occasions he had reached and pointed beyond the racism of the Israel of his day. The experience of the day of Pentecost endorsed this for the new Church. Paul's experience reflected this dilemma. He was 'of the people of Israel, of the tribe of Benjamin, a Hebrew born of Hebrews' (Phil. 3.5), but although he had no reason to be ashamed of his ethnic identity, it was no longer for him the basis of his human status which was now 'in Christ', in whom 'there is no such thing as Jew and Greek'. (Gal. 3.28, NEB).

There is a clear indication in this experience that the affirmation of one's corporate/tribal identity is an essential element in individual identity, in human development and therefore in human community; but that if and when such an affirmation demeans others, it becomes demonic and must be transcended and superseded in favour of an authentic wider common humanity. When an ethnic group is in a minority position and is vulnerable to the destruction or erosion of its identity, it is of great human importance to enable it – if its members wish, and not all necessarily do – to sustain its community viability. But if such an ethnic consciousness then moves on to pose a threat to other groups, a dangerous threshold is crossed.

At the same time, to speak of a plural society implies very much more than diversity; the puzzle of pluralism is the question: How can incompatibilities coexist? Pluralism in Britain today – coming as something of a shock in what has long been a comparatively homogeneous society – has many dimensions. It is much more than ethnic pluralism, though that may imply deep differences of culture and religion; there are groups holding and propagating irreconcilable differences of ideology and political programmes, a plurality of lifestyles, of ethical norms, while behind them lies a fundamental philosophical pluralism, posing the profoundly unsettling question: Does the universe cohere in an ultimate unity, or are we in a 'polyverse' with no integrating principle?

We find 'the other' threatening. Homosexuality arouses hostility because it arouses fears in our psyches, questioning our own security. There is no surer way of raising community consciousness than focusing fear and hostility on an outside threat. The uninvited presence of travelling people or a 'peace convoy' arouses passionate opposition from respectable citizens. The phrase 'these people', whether used of those with handicaps or any other minority, is a sure sign of resistance to pluralism. Richard Sennett has drawn our attention to the obsession of suburban society with the removal of any non-conformities, any environmental disorder – yet, as he reminds us, it is those very elements of disorder which present us with the opportunities to grow to maturity.[3]

The puzzle and pains of pluralism were never far below the surface of the pages of *Faith in the City*. It is an inescapable factor in the life of Urban Priority Areas. Our biblical exploration can help us to see that genuine community rests not on a foundation of 'people like us', but on a covenant, explicit or implicit, which embraces all humankind. This lesson transformed the early Church and burst the frontiers of conventional homogeneity. Today in Urban Priority Areas it is the most vulnerable people who are exposed to the severest tensions. This makes it all the more important for the Church, locally and nationally, to have not only clear policies which address these issues, but also a supporting presence within the community. This requires something much deeper than conventional liberal tolerance which regards a supposedly 'neutral' state as holding the ring. In fact, the dice are loaded decisively against the weak. The State is now revealed as a powerful element in causing the deprivation of Urban Priority Areas.

The task of the Church in a plural society is thus a double one: both to support and often radically criticize and work to change the framework which holds a plural society together and yet also to be an active protagonist for minority-group positions, not only or primarily with regard to the community of faith, but with regard to issues of justice and truth. These two roles may be distinct, but at root are one. Upholding the framework may not appeal to some Christians, but it derives from our understanding of God's covenant with the whole of humanity; and only those who are privileged to live in a relatively stable society can afford the luxury of disregarding the risks of the social disintegration which ensues when all acceptable social control breaks down and the bully boys run all over the weak.

Many of the elements in British society which together sustain the common framework are under social pressure. John Habgood, the Archbishop of York, discusses these factors in his *Church and Nation in a Secular Age*.[4] The monarchy, Parliament, the Common Law tradition, the Civil Service, networks of conventions, assumptions and unwritten understandings, assertions of national identity, good neighbourliness and citizenship – and, one could add, the media – most of these factors need constant and sometimes radical modification, and any Church which sees beyond being a sect must work at the task of challenge, debate and upholding 'the common good' and affirming the common life.

In a religiously plural world, our affirmation must be that the ultimate purpose is for the entirety of the human community to be transformed into a fulfilled humanity; for Christians, this can mean only 'the likeness of the Son of Man'. But this vision does not imply that this must be through the Church. A hope for a common transformation implies radical changes for all, but, in the light of the biblical tradition, most radical of all for the community of faith.

The demand for right-dealing

A further aspect of the covenant which sustained the community of the Bible was the demand for 'right-dealing' – in the Old Testament, 'justice'; in the New Testament, the 'works' inspired by love. The Hebrews lived by a law which they believed to be divine and totally binding upon them, and the Church remained committed to the importance of law in society. For the Hebrews, God was engaged in an active process of putting things right, and he willed his people to work out their relationship with him through right-dealing in the community. To this end, people in different walks of life, who were able to articulate God's word to their community, were accepted as recipients of divine instruction (Torah), teaching and interpreting 'the helpful directing will of the God who conducted his people through history'.[5] In time, of course, the basic instructions were codified, first in very ancient formulations, from the Ten Commandments onwards, and later expanded and edited into the books of the Pentateuch which formed the core of the sacred writings.

The heart of righteousness, the standard by which right-dealing was to be judged, was not conformity to an abstract norm (justice), but was 'judged wholly from the point of view of faithfulness to a relationship'. 'Every relationship brings with it certain claims upon conduct, and the satisfaction of these claims, which issue from the relationship, and in which alone the relationship can persist, is described by the term *tsedeq* (righteousness).'[6] As von Rad sums it up: 'Jahweh issued the orders of life which alone made men's life together possible. His commandments were not indeed any absolute "law", but a kindly gift rendering life orderly.'[7]

Such an understanding of justice required, above all, response to the needs of those who were least able to voice their needs, the fatherless, the widow, the stranger, and, over and over again – in virtually every strand of the tradition, historical, prophetic and in the Psalms and wisdom literature – the poor. This was the point at which the moral imperative of Yahweh lifted the idea of aboriginal community based on common origin or ethnicity to a concept of community based on the conscious moral acceptance of the obligations of human relationship. Put in abstract terms, the requirements of justice superseded the claims of natural kinship or territoriality, requirements that were given a new force and urgency by the teaching of Jesus.

Covenant, contract and the common good

What light does this throw on the *'grave and fundamental injustice'*[8] which *Faith in the City* found existing in British society today? On what basis should society adjudicate between competing claims, between wants and needs? If we start from the Enlightenment assumption that society is an aggregation of competing individuals and collectivities, we face the war of 'all against all'. On this basis, rational allocation of resources rests on the assumption 'that economic and social relationships could be treated like the relationships of physical sciences,' requiring 'that they be reducible to undifferentiated elements which are equivalent and can be substituted one for another'.[9] As Bishop Lesslie Newbigin has said: 'If to be a truly human person is to be an autonomous individual, depending on no charity but demanding and defending one's rights, then to receive charity is indeed to lose dignity.'[10]

But what is the alternative? Benevolent paternalism is an option much favoured in Britain, but it will not do, in spite of apparent consonance with some aspects of the biblical pattern. For paternalism leaves all the power in the hands of the rich and powerful, at whose discretion resources are shared – or not. It also sets charity against justice if charity is experienced as a demeaning handout to a suppliant. Tom Paine, in his *Rights of Man*, drew attention to the rights of the weak (which could be inferred from but were not expressed as such in the biblical traditions). The articulation of such rights properly provides a countervailing power over against the strong.

Does this get us towards a framework in which right-dealing can be established in a plural, post-Enlightenment society? Jürgen Moltmann has written:

> How can the humane character of the human community be measured? I believe by the *measure of justice*. A human community is 'humane' when it is perceived as just and when it is just. But what then is justice? According to our western perception, justice on the material level means 'to each their own'. According to the biblical understanding, justice is communal faithfulness and means on the personal level: the recognition and acceptance of other people. Mutual acceptance and recognition creates a just society. The highest form of justice is the law of compassion through which rights are created for those without rights. This is the justice of God,

'who executes justice for the oppressed' (Psalm 146.7). It is the 'preferential option for the poor', as the liberation theologians say.[11]

How is this vision to be embodied in a social system? It will be by acceptance of the basis of society as community. For any community to function humanely, two things are needed. Not only must space be found for ways to meet needs based on what a person requires *in order to be human* (to be treated differently, and with personal warmth) – something that cannot be legislated for as entitlement nor required as of right. But there must also be congenial structures and institutions, often properly acting impersonally, treating 'all alike' and embodying a serious concern for structural justice, giving scope for voices to be heard and leverage achieved by those most at risk of exclusion.[12]

This involves the acceptance of what Professor Ralf Dahrendorf calls 'the social contract' – 'the fundamental assumption of modern, free societies which is that everyone without exception is a citizen with entitlements common to all'.[13] This, in the common language of public debate, is an implicit covenant, enshrining the essential implications of the pattern of God's covenant with his people, and the relationships that went with it.

The context of community, with reciprocal obligations and rights for all members, and a basis of belonging together with mutual respect, provides a foundation upon which the apparently insoluble confrontations of a society based largely on conflicting rights, and the unacceptable inequities of a society based on paternalism, market forces or acquisitive individualism, can be approached with hope. If society is experienced as community – with differences of institutional expression at local, regional and national levels – there is at least an expressed will that no individual or group will suffer exclusion from participation in the processes of creating and sharing in the benefits and costs of the common life. It was the denial of such an implicit social covenant that led to the conclusion of *Faith in the City* that the essence and the pain of the 'grave injustice' of Urban Priority Areas lay in the experience of exclusion.[14] This is the central issue in British life today, and has major implications for the task of the Church in working for changed social attitudes and structures in British society.

COMMUNICATION AND THE COMMON LANGUAGE

The word *koinos* in the Greek New Testament means 'common' in the sense of 'shared', and also 'common' in the sense of 'commonplace', 'not special'. In a Jewish context, this meant 'not holy', 'profane', 'unclean', 'unwashed', 'dirty'. We must note that the Old Testament understanding of holiness was 'belonging to God' or 'set apart to be used for and identified with the loving purposes of God', as distinguished from people and things in general or common use, which were, by definition, defiled, dirty. This distinction had dominated Jewish culture for centuries.

Now, at a stroke, as a result of the life and death and risen life of Jesus, not only was the common life redefined, but the world itself had a radically different meaning: the common is 'holy', in principle belonging to God, designed to be identified with his purposes of love. The creation is not of itself evil, polluted; the common people, 'the great unwashed', *all of us*, are to be seen as God's holy people. One implication of this new perception was spelt out clearly in the story of Peter's vision in Acts 10: the old distinction between Jew and Gentile was obsolete, both would be members on equal terms of the new community. But another implication was more far-reaching. *Nothing* was now to be called 'unclean'. The Church was no longer to exist by excluding certain aspects of life and experience from view. *Everything* was now to be exposed to the sanctifying influence of the Spirit.

A common language

I have argued that there can be only one valid basis for the Church as an organization to be involved with purposeful intervention in the common life of the community, whether local or wider: that basis is our conviction of a divine covenant with the whole created order and that Christ is Lord of all. If this is what we believe, a further step is necessary: to accept that this universal sovereignty can be generally expressed only in language which is common to all – in the categories of discourse which carry shared meaning in the common life. Although this conviction of God's universal sovereignty is firmly grounded in Scripture and Christian experience, it cannot be effectively or generally communicated to the community-at-large in the language of faith which has been developed over the centuries within the Church.

It is inevitably difficult for those most committed to the community of faith and the language of faith – especially perhaps clergy – to accept such a statement. The temptation is to dismiss talk of using the common language as merely an attempt to water down or attenuate the proclamation of the kerygma to make it acceptable to 'modern man'. But a few moments' thought should be enough to provide reassurance that this is not so. Of course, the proclamation of the fullness of the faith to all inquirers is intrinsic to the nature and mission of the Church, for there are many who have ears to hear and to respond; as Christians we must always be ready to give reasons for the faith that is in us. For us, it must be clearly asserted that, for discourse about the common life in a plural society, the religious language of Christian faith cannot be the common language of discourse.

This is necessary, not only because the language of faith cannot normally be 'heard', but also, more importantly, because we know Christ to be Lord of the common life, and not only of the Church; we not only can, but must, articulate his word to the community in a language which the whole community – and the constituent parts of it – share. Of course, different groups in the community use their own 'languages' in the networks, the different worlds of discourse, of technology, culture or class. But these, for our purposes, can be regarded together as special elements of the common language of the community at large. The message of the community of faith has to be conveyed in the common tongues of the community and not in the esoteric in-language of the ecclesiastical sub-culture. This is not a retreat from authentic Christian proclamation; *the common language is the only medium of exchange which has validity in the community*, and the Church can be confident that the currency in which it is paid bears the watermark and image of Christ. We know that the common, including the common language, is now holy – belonging to God.

To speak the common language does not involve accepting all the assumptions of our culture. If we are true to the deepest human experience, we face up to reality, knowing that 'the way things really are' is consonant with our biblical understanding and with Christian paradigms. As Alan Gawith has recently reminded us, 'secular realities have major life-shaping influences and life-and-death-affirming forces. Therefore to take them seriously is a primary theological necessity: they cannot be side-stepped, ignored or demeaned in God's name, although they may be opposed, challenged or transformed in that name.'[15] It is as well to remember that the Greek word *aletheia* is translated both as 'reality' and 'truth'.

A common language does not therefore commit us to any naive optimism about human nature. We can share the common understanding that of course our heritage is deeply flawed, that singly and together we add to the wrong and the pain. But the flawed heritage is in the context of an original blessing, a primacy of the good creation.[16] In sharing our convictions about the realities of life with the community at large, for example through the media, if we want to be heard we may find ourselves using such expressions as the common good, stewardship, integrity, faithfulness, justice, altruism, and a commitment to reality – virtues and experiences which undergird any human community. In teasing out the meaning and implication of such terms as responsibility, mutuality and exchange we will draw from and feed back into the language of faith.

This is the 'implicit theology' which must be the assumption of any serious engagement by the Church in community.[17] It does not, of course, replace the explicit theology which involves thinking about the language of faith within the community of faith; but in the context of the common life of the community at large our language must be that of implicit theology, not only with, as Alan Gawith suggests, 'the hint of transcendence'[18] but always with a radical openness to 'the Beyond in the midst'.

The ambiguous word 'secular' is a hindrance in this discussion and is best dropped, for it carries the inference that the secular is not only (properly) outside the ecclesiastical realm, but also (misleadingly) outside divine concern. This is a confusion which has nullified so much of the discussion in Christian circles of Bonhoeffer's seminal insights, and has led to something of a loss of nerve, 'a closing of the ranks in the face of the growing threat of secularism' and a retreat into ecclesiastical concerns, turning our back on the community, almost as though we were not part of the common life; as if 'the community' started outside the lych-gate.

An instructive parallel to community work may be found in the experience of Industrial Mission. The report *Industrial Mission – An Appraisal* describes how Industrial Mission 'practitioners have often found themselves apparently forced to choose between not speaking of God at all and speaking of God in slogans imported into the world from the spheres of preaching or academic theology'.[19] Meanwhile,

> those responsible for the parochial and congregationally-based ministry, with its own pressures, were profoundly unconvinced by a notion of mission without 'naming the Name', eliciting a personal response to Jesus Christ, and encouraging those who heard of Him to participate in the worshipping life of the local Christian community. Furthermore, such a notion appeared to undermine the assumptions and practice of their own ministry, even while it depended on their ministry for its financial support.[20]

If those who are professionally most closely committed to the mission of the Church are locked into the use of the language of faith, who is helping lay people in the common life to communicate the divine project in the common language?

This dilemma is near the heart of any understanding of the practical commitment of the Church to involvement in community.

Jesus set us the pattern of using the common language of his community to communicate the deepest truth of life. In the centuries since, the Church has developed a religious language in which elaboration has smothered resonance. Yet the book of Acts is at heart the story of the Holy Spirit communicating across barriers of language, culture and tradition. Ecstatic exuberance was not the heart of the matter, although it involved the deepest emotions. Nor was it a matter of intellectual acrobatics, although it engaged some of the ablest minds in history. Communication was personal, corporate and caring, because it took place within a community which was experienced as given.

Clearly it is our calling as the Church to develop a common lifestyle which expresses the divine project as unambiguously as we know how. Some of these implications were set out in *Faith in the City*. If the Church is to be a sign of the Kingdom, subsidiary to and pointing towards the Kingdom, it is the responsibility of the institutional Church to encourage those groups who give their lives and devote their energies, for the sake of the common good, in conscious solidarity with Christ. Some of these groups are communities sharing common residence or formal commitment.[21] Some are engaging with specific issues or involved with the people of a specific neighbourhood or wider community; many of them have 'Christian' or 'Church' labels.

But such a commitment will by no means exhaust the responsibility of the Church in the wider community of which we are part. This is not only a matter of the intellectual or verbal communication of ideas. Ruth Etchells has said, 'Somehow we have to tell it out by living it out that the whole of life is redeemed and holy.'

CONFLICT

The prophets

For the people of Israel, community was process, and often conflictual process. It was experienced in the flow of human interaction, and was not a concept to be analysed. Community was not an idealized, static norm. Nor was it a cosy mutual *bonhomie*. It was a tumultuous and often painful common journey involving conflicts, violence, uprooting. It was about a people defining their ethnic purity and identity as holiness – belonging to God and therefore to each other – separated from and over against their neighbours. At the close of the Old Testament, the process, they knew, was unfinished; the vision was held out to them that their destiny was to pioneer a path for humankind.

A vital constituent in the process was the phenomenon of prophecy. The term 'prophet' in Jewish tradition and in the New Testament is used to describe a very much wider category than the subjects and authors of the prophetic books. Many of the great figures of the tradition were referred to as 'prophets', notably Moses (Deut. 34.10).

This indicates that most of God's spokespeople were *insiders*: advisers to the royal court; those administering social control through the institutions of society; priests regulating the ritual processes of cleansing, restoration or exclusion; judges or elders dispensing justice at the gate – in other words all those attempting to ensure that 'divine wisdom is *continuously* embodied in the holy community through its succession of recognised teachers'.[22]

But because it is God's purpose that power should be used to establish justice, then the holders of power must be committed to use power as 'holy' – belonging to God. In case they use it for other ends, they must be subjected to scrutiny and accountability when they are corrupt or unjust. Hence the need for other prophetic spokesmen who stand within the community but outside the systems of the Establishment – *outsiders* who have the courage and insight to speak words of judgement, warning and correction.

The prophets whose names are associated with the prophetic books of the Old Testament were notable spokesmen (the records speak mostly of men, though there were faithful, wise and articulate women, too) with a rare sensitivity to the inner voice of God, recalling their contemporaries to 'the quality of life known in the Exodus community with which God made his covenant'.[23] The prophets knew that whatever a community worships is the driving motivation of its life; idolatry was a betrayal of the covenant and courted disaster.

Deliverance from the abuse of power and corruption could not be achieved without conflict. The example of Jeremiah may illustrate the point. Called in his youth to be God's spokesman to his people, he lived through tumultuous times when the Chaldean armies besieged and eventually captured and ravaged Jerusalem. He spoke out against the policies of the king and his advisers, against the false prophets and against the priests who had betrayed the covenant.

He suffered rejection by his own family, denunciation by the Jerusalem mob, was put in the stocks, flogged, imprisoned in mud, even sentenced to death; he survived to witness the fall of the city in 586 BC, and eventually to be taken by force with a party of refugees into Egypt where he died.

Nevertheless, throughout his life, Jeremiah never ceased to affirm his solidarity with his community. Although saying hard and unpopular words against them, they remained 'my people' (for example Jer. 8.18—9.2). 'Remember', he reminds God, 'how I stood before thee to speak good for them, to turn away thy wrath from them' (Jer. 18.20). It was because of his commitment both to the Lord of the community and to the faithless community itself that Jeremiah was impelled to confront the people and suffer the consequences.

The Church

The same tension between commitment to God and commitment to the community soon made its appearance in the early Church. The Acts of the Apostles and some of the letters of Paul tell of conflicts which caused bitter divisions. There was a sharp confrontation and conflict between Peter and Paul (referred to in Gal. 2.), and tension between the Jerusalem church and Paul. James Dunn writes of 'a Jewish Christianity which had aligned itself so firmly with its Jewish heritage and which had set its face so firmly against Paul and the law-free Gentile mission',[24] that 'it is evident that there was a much deeper divide between Paul and the Jewish Christianity emanating from Jerusalem than at first appears'.[25]

The pattern of resolution of these conflicts in the New Testament follows something of the same paths as in the Old. Paul and Barnabas, after their personal confrontation concerning John Mark – 'the dispute was so sharp that they parted company' (Acts 15.39, NEB) – followed a prudent course of separation. Relations with the Christian community at Jerusalem were maintained through the acceptance of the pain of a willingness to accept and respect each other. But, in the words of Stephen Sykes, 'from the start there was a diversity of interpretations of Jesus' teaching . . . Internal conflict inheres in the Christian tradition, even in its earliest forms.'[26]

Community and conflict

Every society has to hold a balance between consensus and conflict. The concept of community, in current discussions of British urban life, tends to carry strong overtones of a consensual approach. Upholders of community appear to emphasize what contending parties have in common, to minimize or suppress confrontation, thereby, it is suggested, supporting or perpetuating situations which may be unjust. Community thus too easily becomes associated with an Establishment point of view, opposing what may be necessary (but painful) change and colluding in collective or individual wrongdoing. As Jürgen Moltmann says, 'the community is always conservative'.[27] Our biblical exploration, however, must serve as a sharp corrective to any idea that community precludes conflict. We have noted from both Old and New Testaments (notably the prophets and the apostles) that a profound experience of community, far from suppressing conflict, actually made it necessary for conflicts to be brought into the open. The ways in which conflicts were handled are an indication of how right relations can be enhanced and restored.

The warm, soft, unconflictual feel of the community model of human togetherness makes it particularly congenial to the Church. As *Faith in the City* made clear, 'We have little tradition of initiating conflict and coping with it creatively. We are not at home in the tough, secular milieu of social and political activism.'[28] Perhaps the religious conflicts of the 17th century scarred the English psyche too deeply. Certainly, conflict is held to run counter to the whole ethos of the Christian faith. There are prudential considerations, a fear of arousing passions which may get out of control, liberal assumptions of easy, 'rational' consensus. Most crucial, however, must be the fear that if we take issues of justice seriously to the point of confrontation, we will be challenging the holders of power, exposing ourselves to risk, and we may lack sufficient courage, confidence, knowledge, political skills or collective support to embark on a course that would be bound to lead to divisiveness and the alienation of support in the Church.

But such considerations must be held up to the mirror of the biblical experience of community. It was *because* the prophets of Israel were inescapably part of the holy community that they were impelled to raise the contentious issues of the abuse of power and the oppression of the poor that God had laid on their hearts. It was *because* Peter and Paul were wholly committed to the community of the early Church that they could not escape the responsibility of challenging the views which they knew were not faithful to the new covenant relationship with Christ. Their confrontations were not betrayals of the community, they were necessary expressions of it.

Resolving conflict

Most differences in society are resolved by some accommodation between the parties, agreed or imposed on the assumption of a greater 'we' – that neither side wishes to destroy the other; this is the assumption of community, that in the last resort we all belong to each other and have to live and work together tomorrow. But when the most vital issues are at stake, or when an individual or a group are in the grip of an almost pathological obsession, there is a will utterly to destroy the other side, to obliterate their humanity. (This was the philosophy of *Totalkrieg*, total war.) This is a violation of the implicit covenant with all humankind – in the language of faith: the Noachic covenant and the new covenant in Christ. It is a denial of the fundamental community embracing all humankind and the whole created order. Unless there is some internal change, the relentless outworking of such implacable forces within the space given to us which we experience as freedom is what the Bible calls the wrath of God; the pursuit of remorseless victory carries within it the seeds of ruthless retaliation.

Human experience shows that there is only one way to break the self-perpetuating cycle of power conflicts: it is the use of power in a transformative way. When groups (or individuals for that matter) are locked in sharp conflict, at some point – perhaps even at the moment of victory – an initiative is taken, a nettle grasped, a point conceded, forgiveness extended, an apology made, a compromise suggested, which reaffirms the greater 'we' of community. Such initiatives, however, always carry an element of risk: the others may take advantage, a precedent may be created, one's position seriously weakened, the initiator may be discredited: *one immediately becomes vulnerable.* This vulnerability, however, opens the way for a resolution of the conflict which enables the parties to emerge without humiliation and with a future open to a positive relationship. It is the readiness to accept such vulnerability that embodies in everyday situations the transformative power that is the only way conflicts can be healed and changed from within. In the language of faith, this is the mark of the Lamb, with the marks of slaughter upon him, wholly vulnerable, but yet 'at the heart of the throne' (Rev. 7.17, NEB) embodying the ultimate divine power in the transformation of human community (Rev. 5.12–13).

In contemporary urban Britain, the traditional rhetoric of 'class' divisions carries less and less conviction; nevertheless, very sharp conflicts of interest and differences of social status still exist. Violence lies not far below the surface. If the Church is to be faithful to the human communities of which we are part, it falls to us to be faithful to the relationships of the implicit divine covenant with humankind, and therefore to express our solidarity with those who are suffering oppression. But this implies the painful consequence that we have to accept the vulnerability inevitable in the resolution of any conflict.

COMMUNION

The new common human status which had been realized in the Church at Jerusalem at and after the experience of the Holy Spirit at Pentecost was celebrated not only by meeting constantly to hear the apostles teach, and to share the common life, holding everything in common, but the focus of the whole *koinonia* with the risen Christ and with each other was in meeting 'to break bread and to pray'. 'Breaking bread in private houses' they 'shared their meals with unaffected joy' (Acts 2.42, 46, NEB).

But there was more to it than that. John A. T. Robinson, in his seminal study *The Body*, has helped us to take the force of the concept of solidarity in Paul's thinking. All humanity is bound up together in solidarity of the flesh (*sarx*) – not as meaning 'physical', but 'man, in the solidarity of creation, in his distance from God'. The work of Christ has been to bring about a new solidarity in the body (*soma*) which 'stands for man, in the solidarity of creation, as made for God'.[29]

> The resurrection body signifies . . . the *solidarity* of the recreated universe in Christ. It is none other than the Body of Christ in which we have a share.[30]

> In so far then as the Christian community feeds on this body and blood, it *becomes* the very life and personality of the risen Christ.[31]

> The building up of the Church is not the gathering of an elect group *out of* the body of history, which is itself signed simply for destruction. It *is* the resurrection body of history itself, the world as its redemption has so far been made effective. 'The open consecration of a part marks the destiny of the whole.'[32]

Faith in the City was unequivocal in the following statement:

> Ultimately it is only an absolute commitment to our solidarity one with another, a recognition of the importance of all forms of collective action for the common good, and a passionate concern for the rights and well-being of those least able to help themselves, which can redress the balance of the excessive individualism which has crept into both public and private life today.[33]

Scripture constantly reminds us of the focal importance of the shared meal as the most significant expression of community: the Passover and the breaking of bread. For the earliest Christians table-fellowship was both a sign of taking common bread and wine, and a sign of the most intimate fellowship. It consummated, as it were, the profound sharing in the divine life, and in human life, which expressed not only the person of Jesus but the experience of the Kingdom which he embodied and for which he died.

As John D. Zizioulas has summed up the experience and reflection of the early Church: 'There is no true being without communion.'[34] 'The being of God could be known only through personal relationships and personal love. Being means life, and life means *communion*.'[35] This may help remind us that there are not two processes – first an inner spiritual communion and subsequently a practical 'application' in sharing with other people. It is a single, integrated awareness – one which has its ultimate theological basis in the doctrine of the Trinity itself. God is a 'community' of three persons who are fully individual only in their relationship with one another.

This communion does not imply a mystical absorption as drops of water into the ocean of divinity. Communion in the biblical tradition is about relationships between Persons and persons, even across the gulf of Creator and creatureliness. This distinction remains a fundamental issue in relation to Hinduism and Buddhism in the inter-faith dialogue of our plural world.[36]

Perhaps for those who are purposefully involved in community life the heart of the matter is a conscientious acceptance of the givenness of the common life and our place in it – not in a spirit of fatalistic resignation, but with thankfulness for the immense potentiality in every person and every situation, and the shared power to act in hope. Even though we come with common, dirty hands, the thanking is the blessing in the biblical tradition. As we enter ever more deeply into the limitless, open mystery, we find ourselves taken into the cosmic process of transformation which is luring us, and the whole creation, into the new life of the divine community.

Notes

1 The Archbishop's Commission on Urban Priority Areas, *Faith in the City* (Church House Publishing, 1985), 3.22.
2 D. E. Jenkins, *The Contradiction of Christianity* (SCM Press, 1976), pp. 14–16, italics as in the original.
3 R. Sennett, *The Uses of Disorder* (Penguin Books, 1971).
4 J. Habgood, *Church and Nation in a Secular Age* (Darton, Longman & Todd, 1983), pp. 33–49.
5 G. von Rad, *Old Testament Theology*, vol. 1 (Oliver & Boyd, 1962), p. 91.
6 ibid., p. 373, quoting H. Cremer.
7 ibid., p. 374.
8 *Faith in the City*, p. xv, italics as the original.
9 P. Marris, *Meaning and Action* (Routledge & Kegan Paul, ²1987), pp. 120–1.
10 L. Newbigin, *The Welfare State – A Christian Perspective*, The Gore Memorial Lecture, delivered in Westminster Abbey, November 1984 (Oxford Institute for Church and Society, 1985), p. 9.
11 J. Moltmann, 'Has Modern Society a Future? – A Christian Vision of Hope', Lecture in Westminster Abbey, 1987, mimeo.
12 See M. Ignatieff, *The Needs of Strangers* (Chatto & Windus, 1984), p. 15 and *passim*.
13 R. Dahrendorf, *The Underclass and the Future of Britain*, Tenth Annual Lecture, St George's House, Windsor Castle (St George's House, 1987), pp. 6, 9.
14 *Faith in the City*, 15.1.
15 A. R. Gawith, 'Towards a Theology of Community Work' in F. Ballinger (ed.), *The Quest for Community* (Diocese of Leicester Board for Social Responsibility, 1988), p. 21.
16 See, for example, M. Fox, *Original Blessing* (Santa Fe, New Mexico: Bear & Co., 1983).

17 The William Temple Foundation's Community Development Group, in collaboration with the British Council of Churches' Community Work Advisory Group, *Involvement in Community* (British Council of Churches, 1980), pp. 93ff.

18 Gawith, 'Towards a Theology of Community Work', p. 21.

19 Board for Social Responsibility, *Industrial Mission – An Appraisal* (CIO, 1988), p. 49.

20 ibid., pp. 48–9.

21 See, for example, Br. Bernard SSF, 'Franciscan Ideals of Community' in Ballinger (ed.), *The Quest for Community*, p. 9.

22 The quotation is from L. S. Thornton; I have been unable to trace the source.

23 E. W. Heaton, *Old Testament Prophets* (Penguin Books, 1964), p. 96.

24 J. D. G. Dunn, *Unity and Diversity in the New Testament* (SCM Press, 1977), p. 257.

25 ibid., p. 254.

26 S. Sykes, *The Identity of Christianity* (SPCK, 1984), pp. 18, 21.

27 Moltmann, 'Has Modern Society a Future?', p. 7.

28 *Faith in the City*, 3.7.

29 J. A. T. Robinson, *The Body* (SCM Press, 1952), p. 31.

30 ibid., p. 79.

31 ibid., p. 57.

32 ibid., pp. 82–3. The quotation is from B. F. Westcott, *The Victory of the Cross*, p. 51.

33 *Faith in the City*, 3.17.iii.

34 J. Zizioulas, *Being as Communion* (Darton, Longman & Todd, 1985), p. 18.

35 ibid., p. 16, italics as in the original.

36 See, for example, P. L. Berger, *The Heretical Imperative* (Collins, 1980), ch. 6.

4

Conservative Capitalism: Theological and Moral Challenges

Raymond Plant and others

INTRODUCTION

In the Christian liturgy we refer to the common good and our common life together. Within the Christian tradition the concept of *koinonia* is central; Jesus poses for us the question, 'Who is my neighbour?' In the Communion service we talk about enhancing our common life and seeking the common good, while in the Bible the notion of the good or holy city is a very salient idea. We cannot say these things seriously without making an effort to envisage what it means for us today to seek the common good and to attempt to build up our common life. *Faith in the City* poses these questions for us in a fundamental way. Unless we see the common good and common life in wholly other-worldly terms, or as relating to the common life only within the Church, we are challenged to think about how they apply to our own wider society today.

The enterprise which we have to undertake to give meaning to these ideas is inherently political, in that there is not one single authoritative answer, whether in theology or politics, to suggest what steps we have to take to build up our common life and to enhance a sense of community. Politics, in at least some dimensions, is a struggle between different understandings of what common life means, and different assessments of how it is to be brought about. As Christians, inheriting the language of community and *koinonia*, we have to struggle to bring our Christian faith to bear upon how we are to think about community in our own day, and the ways in which government may help or hinder the achievement of such a common life. It would be absurd to believe that this could be a simple and one-dimensional process, to believe that we can deduce political imperatives from theological assumptions in any simple and uncontested way, partly because these assumptions are themselves subject to different interpretations in the Christian tradition, and partly because, as we have said, what political demands a sense of *koinonia* makes (even assuming it is unambiguous) is going to be a matter of dispute. But these difficulties and ambiguities do not mean that we can avoid the struggle of trying to think our way through the issues.

In some periods in the history of a society this kind of thinking may be easier than at others, because there may be a high degree of consensus, politically speaking, about what does, and what does not, sustain a common way of life. However, this is emphatically not our position today. Our own society is now marked by quite a high degree of dissent about fundamental political questions which have a bearing on how we interpret the idea of a common way of life and citizenship, and in particular about questions concerning the nature of human freedom, social justice, the desirable level and nature of equality, what resources individuals need to be able to act as citizens, and the nature and role of government itself – even the question of whether community in any substantial sense is something which we should aim at, at all.

Faith in the City poses the question of our responsibility for one another, particularly for our neighbours who are deprived, and about the best way in which these responsibilities can be discharged. This inevitably requires us to consider some of the basic political issues confronting our society, and requires us to struggle with these questions in the light of the best understanding we can get of what our basic Christian values require us to do. This has to be tentative and exploratory and must not mean that we impugn the sincerity of those who disagree with us. We certainly cannot avoid these questions merely by invoking Christ's assertion that we should 'Render to Caesar the things that are Caesar's and to God the things that are God's' (Mark 12.17). This is not an answer to our problems but an invitation to reflect, because what constitutes the realm of Caesar on the one hand and the realm of God on the other is not self-evident. What is the realm of Caesar? Or, to put it another way, the role and responsibility of government is a matter of central political dispute in our own day. 'What is the realm of God?' is also a matter of interpretation, because if we think through our ideas of incarnation and community, they cannot be understood in a wholly other-worldly and supernatural manner. *Faith in the City* is therefore an invitation to think theologically about some of the fundamental political realities of our own day, and the different values which underlie those realities. This is both unavoidable and controversial.

FAITH IN THE CITY AND THE SOCIAL VALUES OF THE NEW RIGHT

The role of government

One of the fundamental political issues of our day, which has a direct impact on issues of urban deprivation and the appropriate response to it, is the development of the belief on the Right[1] in politics, but not wholly confined to the Right, that the role of government both is and should be limited, and that the solution to many of the social problems in modern society is to be found not in government intervention but in providing a greater role for the free market economy, and for private, voluntary, help. Reflection on the issues posed by this development is not taken very far in *Faith in the City*, and it is our belief that a failure to take free market claims sufficiently seriously may undermine the credibility of a theological response to the issues.

In *Faith in the City* there are many references to inequality, social justice and community, and it is precisely in these areas that some of the New Right thinkers and politicians have posed central questions which any plausible social theology has to confront. Let us take one fundamental section from *Faith in the City* and use it as a basis for considering elements of the New Right's view of basic values, a view which has both normative and empirical elements:

> The creation of wealth must always go hand in hand with just distribution . . . There is a long Christian tradition, reaching back to the Old Testament prophets, and supported by influential schools of economic and political thought, which firmly rejects the amassing of wealth unless it is justly obtained and fairly distributed. If these provisos are not insisted upon, the creation of wealth cannot be allowed to go unchallenged as a first priority for national policy.[2]

Many Christians will take this as self-evident, but *Faith in the City* does not take sufficiently seriously the extent to which the New Right actually disagrees with these assumptions. Their arguments are powerful and need to be considered before the theology of wealth and poverty is put on a sure foundation. The currently influential views of the New Right[3] are equally based upon schools of economic and social and political thought which reject precisely the idea of social justice which is in some ways at the heart of the concern of *Faith in the City*. What is this rejection based upon?

Social justice

There are several distinct strands to a critique of social justice which have to be disentangled. However, before embarking on this, we need to satisfy the practical critic that such a concern with these theoretical issues is worthwhile. If we are to think in a principled way, as the New Right invites us to do, about the role and limits of government, then we have to have a clear idea about the nature of the moral demands which a citizen can appropriately make on government. Most people would agree that perhaps the most basic demand is for internal and external defence: externally to prevent or deter external aggression; internally to prevent individuals transgressing rights such as the right to life, to privacy, property and security.

Beyond this, though, there are major disputes, differences which will yield fundamentally different approaches to the role which we think that government itself ought to play compared, for example, with economic markets, personal initiative, and voluntary collective endeavour. What sorts of things should government collectively do, and to what extent is it morally right for government to use its coercive power, for example through the tax system, to make sure that they are done? One traditional answer to this question is that government should seek to ensure social justice, that is to say, an equitable distribution of social resources between citizens in society. This traditional assumption is both mirrored in *Faith in the City* and challenged by the New Right, who regard the pursuit of social justice as a mirage.[4] It is something which government ought not to do, and, in any case, cannot practically do. So at the heart of the social theology of *Faith in the City* is an unmet challenge to one of its central assumptions, and one which goes to the centre of its presumed view about the nature and the role of government.

First of all we shall consider several rather abstract arguments deployed by thinkers and politicians on the Right against what they see as the ideologically illusory pursuit of social justice – arguments which, while abstract, challenge some of our fundamental assumptions about the nature of human freedom, human society, and the duties which one individual owes to another.

Agency and intention
The first argument is that questions of social justice can arise only where there is agency and intention. When a disadvantage is the result of an impersonal or unintended process, then questions of social justice cannot arise. Take for example the following cases.[5] We would not consider that someone who was born with a genetic handicap, such as spina bifida, suffered from an injustice. There is no doubt that such a person suffers from a grave disadvantage, but it is not unjust because it is the result of an impersonal process, in this case the genetic lottery. In the case of an earthquake the same would hold: the earthquake is not the result of anyone's intentional action, but rather the impersonal forces of nature. If a tree blows down on my house and not yours, this is not an injustice but misfortune or bad luck. Again, where a famine is the result of a natural catastrophe, rather than the maldistribution of food, we would be inclined to say that the suffering involved is a misfortune rather than an injustice. All these examples show that for there to be an injustice there has to be agency and intention. Where

deprivation is the result of an impersonal force injustice cannot arise. These points are then used by New Right economists and political theorists such as F. A. Hayek in *The Mirage of Social Justice* and Sir Keith Joseph in *Equality* to argue that injustice cannot occur as the result of a market economy. The reasoning here is based upon the view that the outcomes of free market transactions lack agency and intention and therefore injustice cannot arise out of market operations. In a market, millions of individuals exchange goods and services for their own individual reasons, and at this level each individual acts with agency and intention, but the overall outcomes of such transactions, which mean that some end up with more and some with less, are not and could not be intended. The so-called distribution of income and wealth is not a distribution in the technical sense at all, because no one either individually or collectively intended that any particular distribution of resources should occur. The outcomes of market transactions are the products of human action but not of design: they were not intended or foreseen by anyone.

In this sense, although they embody human actions, markets are much more like the weather in that their outcomes are not foreseen or intended. Hence those who end up with least, and suffer disadvantage, have not suffered an injustice and there is no justifiable moral claim that they can make on society for a rectification for their condition. In the case of an earthquake our response is one of generosity, it is not a response based upon the idea that an injustice has been done. So it is with markets, the poor may suffer, but they have not suffered an injustice. In their assumption that income and resources generally should be distributed in a socially just way, the authors of *Faith in the City* are assuming that the worst-off members of society have a right based in justice for some rectification of their condition. It is precisely this which the New Right thinkers deny, for the reason given above, and this underlies their philosophy of government, namely that government does not play a morally legitimate role if it seeks to redistribute resources to the worst-off members of society.

Appropriate criteria for social justice
There is also a second, more practical, reason at work here. If we assume for the sake of argument that injustice in the distribution of resources can occur as the result of the market mechanism, *we have no way of agreeing on what the appropriate criteria of just distribution could be*. There is no point in invoking the idea of social justice as a guide to public policy if we cannot get clear criteria of social justice which could guide policy-makers, and the New Right deny that such an agreement can be achieved. They point out that there are many possible criteria

for social justice, for example: distribution according to need, to desert, to entitlement, to productive contribution, etc. Policies based upon one or other of these would yield fundamentally different results, depending on which was taken as authoritative. Critics of social justice argue that in a morally pluralistic society we have no clear way of achieving a consensus over which criterion, or mix of criteria, should be the operative one.[6] Most people would want to see a mixed set of criteria which gave weight to considerations, say, of need and desert, but the critic will ask how this can guide public policy, partly because we have no way of weighting in distribution the conflicting claims of desert and need. In any case, even if we had, at a general level, we have no way of adjudicating what people need or what their deserts are. What people count as needs and deserts will differ between the different moral communities in our society and could be adjudicated only by political, or more likely bureaucratic, fiat. Because of the deep moral diversity and pluralism of modern Western societies, there is no way of solving these dilemmas, and the best guide to what people are worth is what others, from their own subjective standpoints, are prepared to pay for an individual's services in a free market. In the New Right's view, ideas about social justice and notions of a just wage, or appropriate entitlement, are at home only in small communities in which there are clear moral values which are accepted as authoritative across society. Within such closed communities the idea of what individuals and groups are entitled to might have a place, and indeed it accounts for the role which 'just wage' theories had in medieval times where there was such agreement in values. However, in the view of the New Right that is emphatically not our position today.

We live in complex societies with ethnic, cultural and religious diversity, and there is no practical way in which detailed agreement about the criteria of justice could be achieved in a way which would be sufficiently cogent and detailed to guide public policy. The market which is based upon subjective evaluation is the only solvent to such distributional dilemmas. In the view of the New Right, those who believe in social justice are pursuing an illusion, but one with bad social consequences, of which two merit attention here. The first, which has been intimated already, means that public policy would have to be highly discretionary. Because we lack agreed criteria, bureaucrats charged with the task of implementing social justice would have to behave in arbitrary and discretionary ways, just because we lack detailed agreement to guide them, and this degree of necessary discretion is incompatible with the rule of law. Second, when government takes on itself the role of pursuing social justice it makes itself the object of resentment by those individuals and groups which do not get what, from their subjective standpoint, they see as their just entitlement. In the absence of agreed criteria of justice, this is inevitable and in the view of such critics accounts for a good deal of the social discontent in Britain in the 1970s when there was a competition between groups for government resources to meet their subjective views of their entitlement. For these reasons government should get out of the business of trying to secure fair shares between people and regions, because we have no agreement on what fairness entails. As Sir Keith Joseph has argued in *Monetarism is Not Enough*, we should be concerned as a society, and through government, about ensuring a minimum standard of provision, not with the will-o'-the-wisp notion of a just distribution of resources.

Freedom

The final argument of the New Right in relation to social justice concerns freedom. One way in which those who believe in social justice have advanced their case is by arguing that the worst-off members of society are rendered unfree by their lack of resources, that poverty is a restriction on freedom.[7] If it is, then it might be argued that the State, as the guardian of individual liberty, has, as a matter of justice, to be interested in the distribution of resources, because those with the fewest resources will find that they have less freedom than the rest of society. Again the New Right rejects this argument, which, if valid, would have set out a distributive role for government in the context of an argument about freedom.

There are two aspects of the New Right's critical approach to this question. The first is to argue that freedom and ability must be clearly distinguished.[8] Freedom is the absence of intentional coercion, but whether persons are able to do what they are free to do is another matter. There is a whole range of things which I am unable to do but which I am perfectly free to do, in the sense that no one is coercing me or preventing me from doing them. I am free to go on a round-the-world cruise; I am free to run a marathon; I am free to enter a monastic order; but I am for various reasons to do with my economic circumstances, my physical capacities and my previous decisions, unable to do these things. We can clearly define when a person is free to do something, namely by seeing whether he is being coerced. But, of course, people are not able to do everything which they are free to do. If I was free only when I was able to do everything which I am free to do, then I could only be free if I were God, that is to say omnipotent – having the ability to do everything which I am not prevented from doing. This is clearly absurd, so there must be a clear distinction drawn between freedom and ability.

Since our abilities are not merely our own personal capacities but also our resources and opportunities, it also follows that there is a clear distinction to be drawn between freedom on the one hand, and the possession of resources and opportunities on the other.[9] Hence, the first conclusion to be drawn in respect of the role of government is that government can secure equal negative liberty, in the sense of securing the absence of coercion to the highest degree possible, by providing and applying to all citizens equally a framework of law which defines those boundaries the crossing of which would lead to coercion. However, because people are not coerced by their lack of resources, there is no duty on government to seek for a redistribution of resources in favour of the worst off in order to secure a more equal distribution of liberty. Indeed the conservative capitalist ideal of equal freedom requires that it should be defined in terms of non-coercion, because if it meant more than that, say equalizing people's abilities and resources, then it could never be achieved. This argument is the main theme of Sir Keith Joseph's book on equality, where he argues, to use his own words, that 'poverty is not unfreedom'.[10] It may of course limit your abilities to do what you are free to do, but that applies in varying degrees to every mortal person. Hence there can be no legitimate moral claim to social justice, in terms of the redistribution of resources, by appealing to freedom.

This argument is backed up in a number of other ways. If we argue that freedom surely requires at least some ability to achieve one's goals, the New Right critics argue in a way parallel to the argument about moral pluralism which we met earlier, namely that we have no agreement about which abilities and resources are necessary conditions of achieving liberty, even assuming (which, as we have seen, they deny) that there is a connection between freedom and ability. They argue further that the outcomes of markets cannot be coercive, because, according to their view of freedom, coercion can occur only through intentional actions and, as we saw earlier, the outcomes of markets are not intentional in the appropriate respect. While the poor may be poor through the operation of the market, their poverty is not the result of an intentional process, and, in any case, because of the difference between freedom and ability, their poverty is not a restriction of their liberty.

The thesis of the New Right therefore raises profound questions about the nature of human values, freedom and justice which are just not addressed in *Faith in the City*. This failure makes it understandable, at least at one level, why the Report received such a bad press on the Right. It failed to grapple with some of the fundamental issues about freedom and justice, appealing only to the Christian tradition without any attempt to think through what a Christian response to such arguments might be. The same applies to its understanding of 'community'.

The nature and value of community

The Radical Right thinkers are very sceptical about the nature and value of community, not just because of the rather slippery nature of the concept but because they see in it a value which is anti-modern.[11] Like ideas of social justice, community is a notion which is at home in small-scale societies, and is very difficult to interpret and clarify in relation to large-scale societies.

The Right is not antagonistic to communities which are based upon voluntary co-operation and shared interests[12] such as clubs and societies of all sorts. Within such societies there may be clearly defined values and codes of conduct for members – the Church would be an example of such a community. But in the view of the Right, these values are authoritative for such communities only because people have chosen them and contracted into them. They are free to join and to leave, and the source of the authority of the community, and of the common good which defines it, is to be found in that consent.

However, when it comes to wanting to see society as a whole in terms of communitarian categories, the Radical Right is very critical. First of all, the demands of such a notion in a large-scale complex society are very obscure, and an attempt to sustain a sense of overall community is antagonistic to modernization and economic progress. The New Right speaks in terms of an abstract society of general laws limiting the opportunity for coercion, rather than of society being seen as itself a form of community. The idea of a community presupposes shared ends and values which are just not there in a modern society. Rather, what we should strive for is a framework of law limiting coercion, within which each individual will be able to use his own abilities to pursue his own good in his own way. This may for any particular individual be a communitarian good, if he chooses to pursue a concept of the good in common with others. However, community and the common good are private values to do with what individuals consent to do or not do with others in society. As such it is of no concern to government.

If there is a common good in society it is not bound up with agreement on substantive values and a common way of life, but rather with that framework of law which secures to each individual the framework to pursue his private ends, and with the market mechanism which is the best institutional mechanism for securing this. So the

New Right is unlikely to be moved by appeals to the beguiling, but almost totally indefinite, value of community. *Faith in the City* does not adequately address this problem.

Free markets and poverty

The final aspect of the New Right's argument which deserves recognition is its alternative to social justice as an expression of concern with the poor.

It would be a travesty of the New Right's position to portray it as being unconcerned with the poor. New Right thinkers are concerned, but in their view ideas about social justice and equality stand in the way of an appreciation of the best mechanism for dealing with poverty: the free market. On their view, the free market will bring about what is called either the 'echelon-advance' or the 'trickle-down' mechanism, whereby what the rich consume today will gradually trickle down to the rest of society over time. The free market will continually raise living standards for all, including the poorest, but in order to work effectively there will have to be quite marked inequalities.[13] It is, in their view, because we have become confused about the nature of poverty that we find this difficult to accept. In their view, there is a sharp distinction to be drawn between poverty and inequality. Markets require inequality: people need incentives to work, to invest, to take risks. But a consequence of this inequality will be dynamism and growth in the economy, which will have the effect of raising the living standards of all, including the poor, over time, because of the trickle-down effect. In their view there is no direct means of helping the poor through public expenditure. This will only add to the burdens of the economy. The best solution to poverty is the indirect one of cutting public expenditure, lowering taxation, deregulating the economy (particularly through the abolition of rent controls and national pay bargaining). Once the economy is deregulated and taxes are cut, the dynamism of ensuing economic growth will lead to an increase in the standard of living of the worst off.[14] This form of indirect caring is the only one available, and they would see the problems of inner cities and poverty in Britain today as the result not of these policies but of sincere but misplaced attempts on the part of governments since the war to solve the problems through increased public expenditure and through the pursuit of social justice.

Any appropriate theological response to *Faith in the City* must address these issues directly. If our theological resources cannot deal with arguments which go to the heart of human freedom, the nature of social processes like markets, the nature of community and indirect approaches to poverty, then we deserve not to be taken seriously by those people, many of whom are sincere Christians, who espouse these ideas at least implicitly.

In the next section we shall consider an initial moral response based upon reflection on these fundamental values.

A MORAL RESPONSE

There are two ways in which the New Right thinkers' views on the market economy can be evaluated. The first is to confront their philosophical arguments in favour of the market compared with political allocations of resources and values. The second is to consider the empirical basis of their claim that the position of the poor will be improved by the trickle-down effect so that, although a market society will involve an increase in inequality, the poor will in fact be better off than under any other alternative. Both of these approaches are important and will form the rest of this part of the paper.

Markets and values

As we saw earlier, the New Right thinkers have a very distinctive view of both freedom and justice, and interpret them in a way which in the case of freedom makes it compatible with the market, and in the case of justice denies the moral basis of the claims of social justice. However, the cogency of their arguments in terms of these values can be doubted.

Responsibility and markets

The conservative capitalist's assertion that the operations of a market might not be foreseeable for individuals may be right, but this statement will not apply to whole groups. Given that for the conservative capitalist the existing set of property rights and resources has to be accepted, because to attempt to reassign them would be an illegitimate exercise of social justice, it is likely that those groups who enter the market with the largest property rights will end up better off, those with fewest, worse off. If this result is foreseeable, it would mean that market outcomes could be regarded as coercive for the worst off because individuals can be held responsible for the unintended but foreseeable consequences of their actions. For the conservative capitalist, because the outcomes of markets are neither intended nor foreseen, individuals have no collective responsibility for others deprived of the results of market transactions, because their freedom is not diminished. But if the results *are* foreseeable – and this is, we believe, an empirical question – individuals do have responsibility for the outcomes as they affect the worst off members of society.[15] If their

78

deprivation is an infringement of their freedom, the State, which even for the vast majority of conservative capitalists is the ultimate guarantor of individual liberty, has a responsibility for it.

Freedom and resources

Yet the conservative capitalist will maintain that this deprivation does not limit liberty, because there is another aspect of negative liberty, namely that freedom and ability, or freedom and the possession of resources, are different things. Clearly, in some respects, the conservative capitalist is quite right: not all forms of inability limit freedom, otherwise I would be truly free only if I were omnipotent.

The answer to this reasoning rests on the definition of a set of basic abilities and associated resources or needs – the failure to satisfy which would restrict freedom because they are related to the capacity for action itself. Without these needs (for example, health, physical integrity, education and a reasonable income) being satisfied, individuals would be unable to do anything at all. With no command over these sorts of resources, they will be unable to act as 'economic agents'. Because the outcomes of free markets cannot secure the satisfaction of these needs for all, that failure can be regarded as coercive. The community thus has a responsibility to secure these needs independently of the market. One way of putting these points would be to argue that the satisfaction of needs is the basis of the equal liberty of citizens. And as the negative liberties, such as freedom from assault and interference, are secured by the State independently of markets, so should the economic and welfare bases of citizenship.

Social justice

The second central issue for the morals of markets is social justice. The New Right concludes that there can be no effective critique of the market in terms of social justice. The only safe guide to what anyone 'ought to have' in the way of income, resources or status is through the impersonal allocative forces of the market where what a person gets is determined by how other people value his goods and services in a free market. This approach leaves valuation in the hands of each individual and avoids the illiberal and bureaucratic consequences of social schemes.

The appropriate response is, first, that injustice is not merely a matter of how something came about, but lies in the response to it. For example, if I can save a child from drowning at no comparable cost to myself, any failure to save the child, even if its predicament was the result of some impersonal force (perhaps the wind blowing it into the water), would be unjust. The logic can be applied to collective action.

Even if the result of the market is impersonal, failure to organize collectively to meet the needs of people disadvantaged by the operation of the market would be an injustice.[16]

Second, the idea of *effective* agency requires a set of basic goods, such as income, health, education and welfare. If these goods can be linked to the negative freedoms secured by legal restrictions on coercion, it is clear that they could form the basis of a concept of distributive justice compatible with moral pluralism. Everyone has to be able to act effectively, whatever his or her moral values; and to secure these basic conditions of action is an answer to the critical arguments of the conservative capitalists.[17]

While this argument defines a class of basic goods and basic needs in relation to them, it does not of itself say anything about distribution. But the link with the idea of the value of liberty offers the clue for a distributive principle. If conservative capitalist assumptions about equality of respect are accepted, together with the kind of view to be found in Hayek that the criteria for saying that one person is more deserving than another are lacking, there are no moral grounds for saying that some people deserve to have more effective basic liberty. In these circumstances, therefore, the welfare goods which define the conditions of effective agency and the value of liberty should be distributed equally, simply because there are no *a priori* moral reasons for any other sort of distribution.

The institutional consequences of this reasoning require close definition. In doing so, we should learn from the 'public choice' critique of bureaucracy developed by the conservative capitalists. In broad terms, the way to meet it is to argue where possible in terms of statutory rights which will minimize the degree of discretion awarded to administrators, and to provide more of these benefits in cash through a direct redistribution of income and wealth. This method puts power into the hands of citizens rather than bureaucrats and welfare professionals, and makes bureaucracies more accountable to democratic machinery.

Rights

One way in which this argument could be presented is in terms of rights. Conservative capitalists will view rights as negative, as the absence of interference and coercion, not as social and economic rights to resources. The conservative capitalist position is that only negative rights are capable of being protected by law and, indeed, are the only sort of rights compatible with the rule of law. Because negative rights are rights to enjoy forbearance, they can always be equally protected by making sure that people abstain from actions which would infringe negative liberties. So, it is argued, the capacity for effective agency cannot be equalized through social and economic rights. If this element is written into the definition of the rights of citizenship, citizens can never be equally free.

There are two responses to this argument. First, that something cannot be completely achieved does not mean that nobody should seek to make some progress towards it. Second, the assumption about equality and negative liberty is flawed. How much protection is afforded by the State to citizens against an invasion of physical integrity or privacy is a matter of judgement, and will vary between groups and classes in society. That equal *negative* freedoms have not been attained does not mean that they should not be sought. The same is true of the *positive* forms of freedom which involve the satisfaction of the needs of agency. These freedoms must be secured outside the market and protected as a right.

Markets and community

The clearest clash between markets and traditional values seems to be in community. These forms of thought have been influenced by rather romantic ideas about community which do not have a very clear application in a modern industrial economy. Many people have thought in terms of a sense of overall community. Yet ideas based on the market, particularly if limited by the values which we have already discussed, can be made compatible with more modest ideas about partial and voluntary communities. If individuals feel a commitment to a particular way of living, these kinds of rights of citizenship outlined above would empower them to form and sustain voluntary communities of all sorts.

The more difficult consideration arises when a valued form of community life is threatened by changes in the market. The best example in recent years is the coal strike. The market for coal dictated pit closures, but the jobs in question sustained a valued way of life. We have to be sensitive to this form of the claim of community, but although a government should not strive to sustain the traditional industrial base of particular communities against market trends, sustaining a valued way of life is a good reason for a selective policy on government investment for new industry. Both traditional conservatives and socialists are bound to be more sympathetic to ideas of community than the conservative capitalist. Indeed, free market economics was born in a reaction against traditional forms of community life. But while Hayek and others see the claims of community as a threat to a dynamic society, socialists and many traditional conservatives could not accept the abandonment of communities which, through no fault

81

of their own, have lost the capacity to sustain their way of life.

We should not be uncritical of communitarian ideas, many of which are nostalgic in origin and have very little to do with an achievable and sustainable way of life in a modern society. Seeking to ensure that individuals have the effective power to create and sustain their own partial communities is a necessary compromise between the vague but beguiling idea of community and the way in which individualism and social mobility has necessarily undermined this ideal in the modern world. In so far as there is a commitment to a common good, it would be found not so much in the ends, goals and values endorsed by communitarians, but in the framework of institutions which secure both the rule of law, and in the institutions and practices which would support freedom, social justice and equality, in the shape described above.

Although this approach is critical of community in an overall sense, and recognizes individualism as a fact of life in the modern world – an individualism heavily sustained by a market economy – it is not unremittingly individualistic. This is so in at least two ways. First, there is the commitment to collective provision (whether in the form of income or services) in order to secure freedom and justice. Second, we recognize (perhaps more realistically than many defenders of markets) that there are limits to markets within any society; there are moral boundaries which markets cross at their peril since they are unlikely to be seen as admissible in some aspects of life. In contemporary British society clear social values appear to militate against turning certain things – the provision of health care and education, for example – into commodities. It may be that the legitimacy of markets in their appropriate domain will depend upon these moral boundaries being sustained elsewhere. This is, of course, an old argument – that free exchange depends upon a background of accepted values and attitudes which themselves should not be undercut by markets if markets are to be sustained.[18]

The moral limits of markets

There are substantive moral limits beyond which we do not want a market mentality to go. The very legitimacy of markets, we argue, depends upon their remaining within these limits. The first form of the argument is that the attitude of rational self-interest – which market operations have to presuppose if they are to operate effectively – has definite limits, otherwise the defence of the free market itself becomes incoherent. For example, it is very difficult to give the self-interested person an answer to the question why he should not seek subsidy, monopoly and other special privileges which, if generalized, would make the market work inefficiently. One could argue with him, of course, that these actions will not benefit society or the maintenance of the market in the long run, but without some restriction on self-interest and some orientation towards a sense of the public good, it is difficult to see how these arguments could be persuasive. Examples of this would include the amoral and self-interested activities of those involved in City scandals in 1987, where self-interested motives rode roughshod over the common values on which a market must rest. Markets themselves thus run up against moral limits. Some shared moral values and some conception of the common good are required to provide an environment in which the market can flourish. Not everything can be made a matter of competition, and the recognition of these limits is a necessary condition for the market to operate legitimately.[19]

The second part of the argument, which has been deployed most recently in Richard Titmuss' book *The Gift Relationship*,[20] looks at ways in which markets can be seen to overstep the boundaries of moral legitimacy and despoil the objects it seeks to turn into commodities. Titmuss' own example is blood for donation; he examines how this altruistically-given gift would be despoiled (and made less efficient) if it became a commodity bought and sold in the market. Titmuss argues that if human tissue does not present a limit to what can be turned into an economic commodity, nothing can. Most people would argue that in the case of buying and selling human tissue – whether blood or body parts – the commercial mentality would have overstepped its limits.

But is there really a central moral difference between selling blood and kidneys, which may be the means to life for others, and selling other medical goods to satisfy the needs they may have? However vague and intuitive they may be, there do seem to be definite moral limits to markets in terms of the commercialization of goods and services central to individuals' life opportunities. Any sensitive defence of markets will make some reference to the general environment within which they operate, because it is very doubtful that markets can secure their own legitimacy: they do not necessarily protect liberty, they are indifferent to any distributional outcome, and they may at some point begin to deplete the moral underpinnings upon which their own operations rest. Not all human values are comprehended in the freedom to buy and sell. Some sense of community and integration is an important ideal – and it is, indeed, one on which the operation of the market, where apposite, rests.

Markets and politics

Finally, a good deal of the thinking of the New Right (in its classical liberal form) on the relationship between markets and political institutions has been very critical of politics and political intervention, seeing politics as often dominated by interest groups, less open than markets, more capable of being dominated by powerful, privileged individuals and groups, with political intervention characterized by necessarily limited information and unintended consequences. In all of these respects markets are superior to politics, securing, in Samuel Brittan's famous phrase, participation without politics.[21]

These fundamental issues require exhaustive examination. Yet, while we recognize that collectivists in general and socialists in particular may have expected too much from political processes, nevertheless we believe that the superiority of markets over politics can be overdone. Two examples illustrate this contention. In each a political dimension is necessary, not to 'solve' but at least to contribute to the solving of problems inherent in the market.

The first example is concerned with what Fred Hirsch in *The Social Limits to Growth*[22] calls the tyranny of small decisions. In a market individuals are free to choose on an individual basis, but the market does not provide an arena or a forum in which either the long-term or the strategic consequences of individual decisions can be considered. So, for example, the outcome of a set of individual decisions may be one which no one would have wanted had it been possible to foresee it.

This point may seem abstract and rarefied, but it is part and parcel of everyday experience. For example, I may live in an area in which there is a corner shop within walking distance which I use for convenience, and a supermarket two or three miles away which I visit with the car for the week's shopping. Prices are lower at the supermarkets as their bulk purchases mean discounts from the suppliers. For any particular individual, obviously, this arrangement seems best for all concerned, but the overall effect of rational individual choice is to drive out the corner shop which everyone found convenient and did not wish to see disappear. Driving the shop-keeper out of business was an unforeseen, unintended and unchosen consequence of rational behaviour in the market. It is an outcome which nobody would have chosen, but it emerges as a consequence of individual choice.

It is very difficult in decentralized markets to take rational strategic decisions which may be important to the overall quality of our lives, and to make choices more important than the small decisions characteristic of the much-vaunted freedom of choice of the market. The example of shops and supermarkets may seem trivial, but it is in essence the one which bedevils the rational provision of public transport, and it would also apply to the consequences of developing private medicine alongside the institutions of the National Health

Service. For example, I may approve of the existence of the National Health Service in a general way, but prefer private medical insurance for myself. If enough people exercise this choice, and given the inelastic supply of doctors and nurses, the demand from the private sector may well put up the price of the services of doctors and nurses in the State sector, thereby either increasing the cost of such services (to me as well, as a taxpayer) or lowering their standards or restricting the services available. This effect may in turn affect the extent of medical innovation in the National Health Service, on which the private sector may also depend, at least in the short term. None of these are consequences I would have chosen if I had been able to foresee them, but they are an unintended consequence of an aggregate number of choices.

These are not arguments against markets as such, but they do go some way towards weakening the hold of the idea that markets are the bastion of choice. Sometimes strategic decisions taken by democratic governments and overriding market considerations may well reflect the strategic choice of individuals rather than the tyranny of small decisions in the market.

The second example, also derived from Hirsch, is concerned with 'positional goods', that is, goods which decline in value the more widely they are consumed. Hirsch's own example is that of education, where the instrumental value of education (that is, what it produces for an individual in terms of economic rewards) declines the more widely education is provided. If there are positional goods, there *must* be a breakdown of the 'trickle-down' effect by which wealth gradually 'seeps' through to all members of society and which defenders of the free market look to as an alternative of distributive justice. Because of the trickle-down effect, they argue, the poor will eventually be richer than they would be under any other alternative, even though economic inequality may increase. The existence of positional goods puts a major question mark beside the trickle-down process because, by definition, such goods cannot trickle down and yet maintain their value. So who is to consume such socially scarce goods? The conservative capitalist will argue (and indeed, given the rejection of social justice, can *only* argue): the people who consume them first. The trickle-down effect is an illusion in which the conservative capitalist, by assuming that there are no genuine difficulties with the supply of goods, seeks to bypass political questions about justice in allocation. Others will argue that because of the necessary limits on the supply of socially scarce positional goods there can be no way of avoiding the positional difficulty of their allocation. Merely to say that those who get their hands on them first have a right to consume them will not suffice

85

unless linked to precisely the same theory of social justice that the conservative capitalist rejects.

There remain problems about the political allocation of resources; indeed, the issue is unavoidable. Thought should be given to improving understanding of the principles upon which such allocations would be made, and the institutions required to make them, rather than pursuing an illusion of a world without distributional dilemmas in which issues of freedom, justice and citizenship are bypassed by the impersonal forces of the market.

AN EMPIRICAL RESPONSE

We have now completed the examination of the moral case for the market and have found it wanting in certain respects in relation to freedom and justice – and indeed as a bastion of long-term choice. We need now to move on to an examination of the empirical claim that the market is in fact in the interests of the poor, because although the market will produce inequalities the echelon advance or 'trickle-down' effect means that the poor will still be better off than they would be under any other alternative.

First of all, what have been the effects of the market-based strategy on the poor in the UK since 1979? In a speech in the early days of the Government in 1979, Reg Prentice, then Minister of State at the Department of Health and Social Security, argued as follows: 'If you believe economic salvation can only be achieved by rewarding success and the national income is not increasing, then you have no alternative but to make the unsuccessful poorer.'[23]

Indicators of poverty

Any kind of test of the trickle-down effect is very difficult given the lack of a clear account of poverty from the market conservative perspective. Sir Keith Joseph talks about capitalism producing a constantly rising minimum standard, but talk of relative poverty is frequently seen as just another way of talking about inequality. All that can be done in the present circumstances is to refer to some of the figures about poverty and allow the reader, on the basis of the evidence, to make up his or her own mind whether the trickle-down effect is producing a constantly rising minimum standard. This has to be considered against the recent statement by the Pay Master General to the Commons, when he said that 'The Government are committed to helping all our citizens share in improved prospects, both in personal incomes and public services. This can only be achieved through the ability of an economy to create wealth.'[24] It is certainly very unclear that this is happening to all our citizens, although it is abundantly clear that it is happening to some.

One way of clarifying the issue is to ask to what extent levels of Supplementary Benefit have kept pace with average incomes, and then to take two measures which seem to be incontrovertible measures of poverty: the number of people on Supplementary Benefit and the number of homeless families.

In Table 1 we indicate the changes in Supplementary Benefit levels from November 1978 to April 1987.

Table 1: Changes in Supplementary Benefit levels November 1978–April 1987[25]

Supplementary benefit	
ordinary rate	
single person	+ 95.5%
couple	+ 95.4%
long-term rate	
single person	+ 94.2%
couple	+ 96.0%
Retail price index excluding housing	+ 86.0%
Retail price index all items	+ 96.0%
Average gross earnings	+136.0%
Personal disposable income per capita	+122.5%

Since 1978 personal disposable income in the UK has risen by 122.5% in money terms and by 14% in real terms. However, Supplementary Benefit levels, compared with incomes in general, have fallen from 61% of disposable income per capita in 1978 to 53% in 1987. So, during this period, the incomes of the poorest groups in society have not kept up their share of the total disposable income in society.

Second, the numbers of people being drawn into Supplementary Benefit, and hence into the group which is *not* sustaining its share in total national income, has increased substantially. This percentage has increased by two-thirds, from about three million in 1978 to about five million in 1987. Of course this only indicates the recipients of the benefits, not those who are dependent on them. By 1984 the number of people directly dependent on Supplementary Benefit had risen to 7,729,000, an increase of 77% since 1979.[26] This figure is likely to have increased considerably since 1984.

If we take homelessness as a basic criterion of poverty, which it would be difficult to deny, whatever the other subtleties in assessing

87

poverty, the figures are also alarming. In 1970 just over 56,000 families were homeless; in 1985 the figure was marginally under 100,000 and is likely to have increased since. Hence on these two measures of poverty – Supplementary Benefit and homelessness – the trickle-down mechanism has just not worked.[27]

Other measures show a similar story, although their interpretation will be disputed because they involve considerations of inequality in relation to poverty. However, if we take changes in the real level of gross earnings for the period 1979–86, we see the following picture.

Table 2: Gross Earnings (pounds per week) Adjusted for Inflation at 1986 Prices[28]

	April 1979	April 1986	% Change
Lowest decile	107.40	111.40	+ 3.7
Medium decile	166.40	185.40	+11.2
Highest decile	262.20	320.80	+22.3

The market is clearly not working in a way to produce a constantly rising living standard for the poor, unless an increase of 3.7% compared with 22.3% for the best-paid is regarded as legitimate.

However, it is not only a matter of the market. It is also a matter of the Government's own taxation policy, which (consistent with the views we have discussed earlier) is an attempt to increase inequality as a basis for economic growth on the principle that the rich need to earn more to work harder, while the poor need to earn less. During the period 1979–86, the Government gave away £8.1 billion in tax cuts and benefits. Here is how these benefits were distributed:

(a) The poorest 6 million taxpayers received 8% of the £8.1 billion.
(b) 20% went to the richest 1%.
(c) 22% went to the richest 5%.
(d) 50% went to the richest 10%.
(e) 66% went to the richest 20% of taxpayers.[29]

Again, the poorest sections of the population are bearing the burden of trying to create an enterprise culture, but, as we have seen, the market mechanism in relation to the numbers thrown on to Supplementary Benefit is not working in the way assumed.

Regional inequalities

As we saw earlier, the market mechanism is celebrated by its adherents because it bypasses questions of distributive justice (and this is clearly seen in the figures already given about the outcomes for individuals), but there is in Britain another example of the way in which the market has undercut issues of distributive equity, namely the outcomes between regions. Certainly, some regions are doing very well out of the freeing of the market; but others are doing very badly. This can be shown in various ways: the unequal distribution of employment prospects; the distribution of average earnings; and the distribution of people on social security benefits (see Tables 3, 4 and 5 below).

Table 3: Regional Unemployment January 1987[30]

% Registered Unemployed

North	16.9
North West	14.3
Yorks and Humberside	13.8
West Midlands	13.8
East Midlands	11.4
South West	10.4
East Anglia	9.3
South East	8.5
Northern Ireland	19.3
Scotland	15.1
Wales	14.3

Clearly, the trickle-down effect of the employment opportunities in the market has been highly unequal in its results. A national government concerned with the futures of all people cannot fail to be worried by these consequences of the free market. The present Government's rejection of distributive policies, however, makes it difficult for them to take to these conclusions by making changes in macro-economic policy and in regional policy.

Similar points are borne out in the table concerning average earnings in relation to regions in the country (Table 4).

Again, the market is producing increased inequalities between the North and the South, and this brings into focus again the issue of the market versus distributive justice. If this trend continues, it is difficult to see how the market can be seen in the long term as a solvent of distributive dilemmas.

The final table concerning regional inequalities is concerned with dependence on social security benefits between 1979–80 and 1983–4.

Again, the regional trend indicating the unequal distribution of the burden of society via the free market is very clear.

All of these figures show cumulatively that the trickle-down mechanism is not working as defenders of the free market hope and

Table 4: Regional Earnings of Full-time Workers[31]
Average Earnings as a Percentage of
South-East Average

Region	1979		1986	
	Men	Women	Men	Women
South East	100.0	100.0	100.0	100.0
East Anglia	88.4	88.0	83.8	83.6
South West	85.2	87.0	82.9	83.7
West Midlands	90.4	89.8	83.3	82.4
East Midlands	89.5	87.3	82.0	81.7
Yorks and Humberside	91.3	86.8	83.0	82.2
North West	91.4	88.4	85.2	85.0
Wales	90.0	89.8	81.8	82.6
Scotland	93.3	88.3	86.5	84.4

Table 5: Regional Dependence on Social Security
Benefits[32]
% of Gross Household Income from Social Security
Benefits

	1979–80	1983–4
South East	9.4	9.7
East Anglia	11.0	15.1
South West	14.2	13.2
East Midlands	10.8	13.5
West Midlands	11.1	15.0
Yorks and Humberside	15.1	16.7
North West	14.0	17.0
North	15.7	20.0
Wales	15.5	19.5
Scotland	12.6	17.1
Northern Ireland	19.3	23.6

that at some point issues of distributive justice between individuals and regions are likely to reassert themselves. It is difficult to see how a government can secure a common sense of citizenship if the market produces such radically unequal outcomes.

A THEOLOGICAL RESPONSE

We now turn to an examination of the connection between the discussion of values which has dominated the paper so far and Christian social thought.

Christian theology is an exploration that is never complete. Its aim is to discover connections between God's self-revelation in Christ and the issues that concern us. In this case theological arguments are brought to bear on the discussion of economic and political theories which make up the ideology of the New Right.

Theology cannot be separated from its social context. What is discovered depends on the attitudes and experience of those who are doing it. Liberation theology, for example, has shown how the gospel speaks to people who are struggling against economic and political oppression. It is a reflection on the experience of the Church of the poor in Latin America. Those involved think that a Marxist analysis helps them to understand what is going on in their societies under capitalism, and their theology reflects this.

This reflection is a summary of the work of two groups of people drawn from all over the Winchester Diocese. One was the Theology Group of the Working Party on *Faith in the City*; the other was an In-Service Training course for clergy. Inevitably we brought our prejudices and our varied experience to these discussions. Many, though not all of us, were clergy. We tried to be aware of the effects of class and education on our attitudes to political issues.

There is a tradition of social theology on which we have drawn. Earlier in this century William Temple,[33] R. H. Tawney[34] and Reinhold Niebuhr[35] explored the connections between Christian faith and social, economic and political questions. Before them there is a long tradition of Anglican social thought stretching back to F. D. Maurice, a tradition which particularly makes links between incarnational theology and social involvement. More recently, Ronald Preston[36] and Philip Wogaman,[37] David Jenkins[38] and John Atherton,[39] among others, have continued the work. They have all contributed to a growing body of ecumenical studies which the World Council of Churches has summarized in calling on Christians to work for a Just, Participatory and Sustainable society (now known as 'Justice, Peace and the Integrity of Creation'). What lies behind this formulation of the task? And what might it mean for us?

Specifically, in seeking help from the tradition of Christian social thought we can identify two prominent strands: one is the emphasis on the Kingdom of God; the other is the emphasis on the incarnation. What specifically may these two emphases have to say to New Right ideology with its redefinition of fundamental social values as outlined in the first section of this paper?

Jesus' proclamation of the Kingdom of God is at the heart of the Christian faith. In the teaching of Jesus about the Kingdom of God, the fundamental theme is life as the good gift of the Creator – a gift

91

given to all irrespective of desert or moral worth or ability: all are of equal value in the eyes of the Giver and are to be treated accordingly. So in the Gospels there is outrage in the society of Jesus' day at the company he kept, at the stories he told, and at the meals he celebrated. The message conveyed through his words and actions was that life is gift for all, to be enjoyed by all. Combined with the message of the Old Testament prophets particularly, we may say that this teaching of Jesus implies a fundamentally egalitarian thrust at the heart of the biblical testimony. The Kingdom of God is good news for the individual, and also good news and challenge in terms of the ordering of society. The Kingdom acts as both judgement of what is and promise of what is to come.

Jürgen Moltmann, a German theologian, has written about the Christian vision of God and the meaning of the Kingdom in modern society:

> The glory of the Triune God is reflected, not in the crowns of kings and the triumphs of victors, but in the face of the crucified Jesus, and in the faces of the oppressed whose brother he became. He is the one visible image of the invisible God. The glory of the Triune God is also reflected in the community of Christ: in the fellowship of believers and of the poor.[40]

This is the paradox of the Kingdom: God's power and rule were seen in the cross above all. We are to see Christ for ourselves among the victims in our own society. Moltmann continues:

> We have said that it is not the monarchy of a ruler that corresponds to the Triune God; it is the community of men and women, without privileges or subjugation. The three divine Persons have everything in common, except for their personal characteristics. So the Trinity corresponds to a community in which people are defined through their relations with one another, not in opposition to one another, in terms of power and possession.[41]

Community lies at the very heart of God. The Kingdom is people drawn into relationship to God and one another in a corresponding community. It is non-hierarchical. It is not oppressive. People find their meaning and value for one another in relationships of giving and receiving. Everyone matters because everyone matters to God.

It is from this vision and from our attempts to live it out that Christians have something to share with the world. Sustained by this hope, Christians are called to work for the transformation of every institution and society, so that they may more adequately express the presence and demand of God's Kingdom. However, the formulation of that demand has to be provisional, because it is God, rather than we, who will complete the work of Christ.

Added to this emphasis on the Kingdom is the emphasis on the incarnation which is characteristic of Anglican social thought; that the life of God was made flesh. This fundamental Christian theme particularly challenges any political ideology that is formulated in an abstract manner apart from the lived experience of individuals and communities. It demands that social values be understood and judged from the perspective of the enfleshed experience of all – and particularly the poor.

Let us apply this to New Right definitions of freedom. As was outlined in the first section, the New Right seeks to redefine freedom as the absence of intentional coercion – and to separate freedom from ability. Thus, on this definition, the poor are not unfree ('Poverty is not unfreedom') even if lack of adequate income and other resources may prevent individuals and communities from sharing in the common life of society. For example, lack of resources may prevent people from ever going on holiday, from enjoying the opportunity to give and receive gifts at festivals, from being able to travel reasonably frequently to visit families and friends, and may result in considerable anxiety about provision of basic necessities. According to New Right political thinking this is not 'unfreedom': the poor, though they may feel unfree, are in fact free! Faithfulness to the principle of the incarnation will lead Christians to resist this theoretical and abstract redefinition of a basic social value, and insist that freedom is defined and understood in terms of the lived, material experience of all – and particularly the poor. So poverty feels like unfreedom and is unfreedom; and in a rich society poverty feels like injustice – and is injustice. This is a way of thinking about freedom that is both faithful to the principle of the incarnation and true to the experience of poor people.

The Christian disciple will want to go further in seeking a definition of freedom which is to do with surrender to the will and service of God, and a voluntary choosing of a life of relative poverty, simplicity and detachment. This is the 'perfect freedom' that the Church is called to live out itself and commend to the world. However, it is an understanding of freedom that depends on freedom being defined in terms of the ability to make real choices; and for these choices to be made, basic economic resources are essential. Policies resulting from a political philosophy that defines freedom negatively, in terms of the absence of intentional coercion, will lead to the denial of basic economic resources and so, for many citizens, very limited opportunities to make fundamental life-choices. The result is a poverty that imprisons and demeans.

Such an incarnational understanding will lead Christians to seek an economic order that produces physical well-being for all, which is part of the gift of life. And the way in which these goods are produced will need to respect human relationships of mutual caring. The work people do is part of their response to the Giver of life and an opportunity to contribute to the well-being of society. The way work is organized and shared, and the way what is produced is distributed, should reflect the fundamental equality of all men and women. Greater social and economic equality is an expression of equality in the sight of God.

The movement from Christian revelation to political action is indirect. It depends on technical and practical judgements about the actual situation and available political alternatives. But there are guidelines available which can assist Christians in this reflection. They are derived from an interpretation of the tradition of thought about God.

The Oxford Conference on Church, Community and the State in 1937 made four criticisms of capitalism as an economic ideology. They were that it has a tendency to enhance acquisitiveness, to create shocking inequalities, to develop irresponsible possession of economic power, and to frustrate a sense of Christian vocation.

The World Council of Churches Assembly at Amsterdam in 1948 repeated these criticisms and added: 'Christians who are the beneficiaries of capitalism should try to see the world as it appears to many who know themselves excluded from its privileges.'[42]

Philip Wogaman concludes his examination of *laissez-faire* capitalism in the light of criteria drawn from Christian doctrine by writing: 'In sum, the miraculous market mechanism may be a good servant, but it is almost certainly a bad master.'[43]

The market needs to be constrained in a social and political system that redistributes resources in the interests of economic equality. Acquisitiveness and competition, appropriate to the market-place, need to be balanced by the values of service and mutual care, which capitalism does nothing to enhance, but tends to undermine. The persistence in Britain of high unemployment and a large minority that suffers relative poverty shows that the earlier criticisms of unrestrained capitalism have not lost their point.

Ronald Preston and Philip Wogaman have produced work that stresses that moral equality in the sight of God needs to find expression in the economic and political structures of society. Human dignity requires that people should be able to participate in making decisions that affect their lives. This includes decisions at the local level of the neighbourhood and at work, as well as at the level of the national and international scene. Not only human dignity requires this; universal sinfulness and self-centredness mean that the exercise of power cannot be left to one person or group in any context.[44]

One implication of this insight is that community development work is vital. This seeks to enable people to work together to shape their local environment. In doing so, they escape the isolation and feeling of powerlessness that poverty and unemployment induce. This is an important means to the common good.

The State should foster the sort of institutions and groups in which power and responsibility can be shared and the seeking of the common good can be entered into at every level in society. This positive role for the State is in contrast to the New Right thinking, which considers that social justice is outside the competence of the State and that social and economic equality is undesirable.

We have emphasized the importance of the incarnation and the Kingdom of God. Now a final comment about Christian teaching on the place of the individual in society, which is an important strand in New Right ideology. Christian teaching has contributed to individualism, including economic individualism, by emphasizing the moral worth and responsibility of each person and their value in the sight of God. Yet the vision of God sets that responsibility within the unity of the human race in the love of God. Whatever the ultimate destiny of humanity, our immediate response to this love has to be made in the context of prayer and worship, work and play, which are activities we share with neighbours. In the Bible the justice of God is always creating community, a people to inherit his promises. The whole creation is the object of God's redeeming work. The expression of this belief in our society will lead us to oppose polarization and to work for the fairer distribution of power and resources.

Notes

This paper was first published in 1988 by the Diocese of Winchester as an occasional paper prepared by the Theology and Social Values Group of the Diocese of Winchester's Working Party to consider *Faith in the City*. In addition to Raymond Plant, the Chairman of the Working Party, the members of the group were Bill Ind (until June 1987), Alec Knight, Ann Lewis, Chris Percy, Richard Wheeler and Patrick Woodhouse.

1 For a guide to recent work by New Right thinkers, see N. Barry, *The New Right* (Croom Helm, 1987); D. Green, *The New Right* (Wheatsheaf, 1987); D. King, *The New Right* (Macmillan, 1987); R. Plant and K. Hoover, *Conservative Capitalism in Britain and the USA: A Critical Appraisal* (Routledge, 1988).

2 The Archbishop's Commission on Urban Priority Areas, *Faith in the City* (Church House Publishing, 1985), 3.13.

3 The views of the New Right are to be found, for example, in the publications of The Centre for Policy Studies, founded by Mrs Thatcher in 1974; The Institute of Economic Affairs; The Social Affairs Unit; The Adam Smith Institute; The David Hume Institute. Important books by New Right thinkers are K. Joseph and J. Sumption, *Equality* (John Murray, 1977); K. Joseph, *Stranded on the Middle Ground* (Centre for Policy Studies, 1975); K. Joseph, *Monetarism is Not Enough* (Centre for Policy Studies, 1976); F. A. Hayek, *Law, Legislation and Liberty* (Routledge & Kegan Paul, 1973–7), 3 vols; M. Friedman, *Capitalism and Freedom* (Chicago, 1962); M. Thatcher, *Let Our Children Grow Tall* (Centre for Policy Studies, 1977); T. Congden, *Monetarism* (Centre for Policy Studies, 1978); B. Griffiths, *Monetarism and Morality: A Reply to the Bishops* (Centre for Policy Studies, 1985); Lord Harris of High Cross, *The Morals of Markets* (Centre for Policy Studies, 1987).

4 This is mirrored in the title *The Mirage of Social Justice*, the second volume of Hayek's *Law, Legislation and Liberty*.

5 This argument is to be found in Hayek's *The Mirage of Social Justice*, in Sir Keith Joseph's *Equality*, and in H. B. Acton, *The Morals of Markets* (Longman, 1971). Sir Keith Joseph argues as follows: 'What renders a particular distribution of wealth fair or unfair is not the distribution itself, but how it arose. Since inequality arises from the operation of innumerable preferences it cannot be evil unless the preferences are themselves evil' (*Equality*, p. 78).

6 See J. Gray, *Hayek on Liberty* (Blackwell, 1981); Barry, *The New Right*; Green, *The New Right*.

7 See R. Hattersley, *Choose Freedom* (Penguin Books, 1987).

8 See F. A. Hayek, *The Constitution of Liberty* (Routledge & Kegan Paul, 1962); Joseph, *Equality*, p. 48.

9 See Joseph, *Equality*, p. 49.

10 ibid., pp. 47ff.

11 See Hayek, *The Mirage of Social Injustice*.

12 See R. Nozick, *Anarchy, State and Utopia* (Blackwell, 1978).

13 See Hayek, *The Constitution of Liberty*; Joseph, *Equality*; Thatcher, *Let Our Children Grow Tall*. See also Mrs Thatcher's election speech reported in the *Guardian*, 13 June 1987.

14 See Joseph, *Monetarism is Not Enough*.

15 For an attempted response to this argument, see Green, *The New Right*; for further discussion, see Plant and Hoover, *Conservative Capitalism in Britain and the USA*, op.cit.

16 For a response, see Green, *The New Right*.

17 For further argument on this, see R. Plant, P. Taylor-Gooby and H. Lesser, *Political Philosophy and Social Welfare* (Routledge & Kegan Paul, 1981).

18 For further argument here, see J. Habermas, *Legitimation Crisis* (Heinemann, 1974).

19 See R. Dale, *Dilemmas of Pluralist Democracies* (Yale, 1983).
20 R. Titmuss, *The Gift Relationship* (Allen and Unwin, 1971).
21 See S. Brittan, *The Role and Limits of Government* (Temple Smith, 1983).
22 F. Hirsch, *The Social Limits to Growth* (Routledge & Kegan Paul, 1977). For further discussion, see R. Plant, 'Hirsch, Hayek and Habermas, the Dilemmas of Distribution' in A. Ellis and K. Kumar (eds), *Dilemmas of Liberal Democracies* (Tavistock, 1983).
23 Quoted in A. and C. Walker, *The Growing Divide: A Social Audit 1979–87* (CPAG, 1987), p. 8.
24 Hansard House of Commons Debates, 6 April 1987.
25 From A. and C. Walker, *The Growing Divide*.
26 ibid., pp. 22–3.
27 ibid., pp. 24–5.
28 ibid., p. 29.
29 ibid., p. 31.
30 From the *Employment Gazette*, Department of Employment, London, March 1987.
31 From *The New Earnings Survey*, Department of Employment, London, 1979–87.
32 From the *Family Expenditure Survey*, Department of Employment, London, 1980–5.
33 W. Temple, *Christianity and the Social Order*, ed. R. Preston (SPCK, 1976).
34 R. H. Tawney, *Religion and the Rise of Capitalism* (New York, 1926).
35 R. Niebuhr, *Moral Man and Immoral Society* (London, 1932).
36 R. H. Preston, *Religion and the Persistence of Capitalism* (SCM Press, 1975).
37 P. Wogaman, *Christians and the Great Economic Debate* (SCM Press, 1977).
38 D. Jenkins, *The Contradiction of Christianity* (SCM Press, 1976).
39 J. Atherton, *The Scandal of Poverty – Priorities for the Emerging Church* (Mowbray, 1983).
40 J. Moltmann, *The Trinity and the Kingdom of God* (SCM Press, 1981).
41 ibid.
42 Quoted by J. C. Bennett in *The Morality of the Market* (Fraser Institute, 1985).
43 Wogaman, *Christians and the Great Economic Debate*.
44 See Preston, *Religion and the Persistence of Capitalism*.

5

Towards a Black Theology for Britain

N. Barney Pityana

'The times are a-changing', the folk song of the 1968 student revolution, found echoes and substance in the song 'We shall overcome', the song of the American civil rights movement. The social revolution of 1968 that so preoccupied the Western university cities of Paris, London, Los Angeles and elsewhere in the United States was an affirmation of alternative values and lifestyles. The civil rights movement was, at heart, an assertion of black humanity. The birth pangs of a new era were often bloody and society was almost at breaking point. But black people the world over did gain new confidence. They came to believe once again in the possibilities of a brave new world.

It is now over twenty years since those heady days. Our context is Britain of the 1980s – the Thatcher era. But the pace of that revolution has hardly abated. It may not always be obvious. It is marked by occasional urban riots. The black presence in Britain need not, however, be totally characterized by negative stereotypes, but constitutes a creative contribution by black people to British social life and culture.

This essay will analyse the characteristics and tensions of this changing Britain and will suggest that this remarkable phenomenon imposes a new theological understanding. It will therefore isolate and make a case for a theological perspective that is grounded in the black British experience.

Secondly, I wish to point to a process of theological development that is dynamic and evolutionary; one which affirms blackness and is open to cultural diversity and acceptance of the enriching contributions of black people to British life. Positively stated, it is my aim to assert the legitimacy of black cultural and social systems of thought and action. There is no value-free system of knowledge. Theological knowledge must likewise respond in faith to the social context of the Britain of our time.

Thirdly, it is my intention to join the debate, from a black perspective, on the theology of *Faith in the City*. The Archbishop of Canterbury's Commission on Urban Priority Areas produced this

98

Report which challenges Church and nation to address the poverty, social decay and deprivation within the urban areas of Britain. It is no secret that since the beginnings of primary immigration to Britain black people have been concentrated in these deprived areas. I shall take a fresh look at the recommendations of *Faith in the City* and test whether they adequately address the problems.

THEOLOGICAL METHODS

Theology is essentially exploratory: the truth about God implicit in the human condition, a dynamic flow of understanding from the known to the unknown. In theology we dig for the life-sustaining values without which all human living would be futile. The method of arriving at the truth about God and his revelation in our world will necessarily lead one to particular perceptions of the social and theological reality.

One can isolate at least two theological methods. First is the view that the doctrines of faith are drawn from a common well and that they are binding on all believers irrespective of their culture or experience. Such truths are said to be universal and timeless and to apply with equal force to everyone at all times: they are unchanging and unchangeable. Perhaps I need to concede immediately that there are certain universal values that human beings hold on to as human beings. It has been said that the Ten Commandments reflect just such a universal moral consensus. Even with these one can't be too absolute. When the Western imperialists sought to impose their own moral absolutes they came to the view that black people were inferior. Part of this seminal racism can be traced back to social Darwinism and the historiography of Victorians like James Anthony Froude.[1]

Second is the view represented by James Cone, which holds that it is the task of theology 'to show what the changeless gospel means in each new situation'.[2] To understand God, therefore, we can hardly start from the givenness of Scripture or tradition. For to do so would be to dislodge theology from the anchor of 'the situation'. Hence a paradigm shift is indicated. The starting-point for all theological exploration is not 'God' or 'the unknown', but is people in their life-situations, exploring, questioning and struggling with life. Remarkably, there is an early theological statement to be found in the Bible – 'This at last is bone of my bones . . . she shall be called Woman . . .' (Gen. 2.23) – which is an exploration of the nature of community, an anthem on solidarity and an inquiry into human origins and relationships. Experience is the constant factor out of which profound questions about God are raised. However, theological inquiry is not so much a digging into the past as an unveiling of the future. Bernard Lonergan expresses such a view in his ninth thesis in *Method in Theology* when he writes: 'The transcendental field is defined not by what we know but by what we can know and ask about'.[3]

This perspective on the future – the unknown or unrevealed – has become the key to the analysis of what may be termed the 'Marxist theology' of the likes of Norman Gottwald and others. But many black people in our time are confronted with a crisis of faith. They have found it expedient to chart a new course of faith and yet they feel part of the same roots that are now being questioned. What they had always understood and accepted, now, in the light of their experience of rejection and alienation, needs to be recast in a different mould.

This second and more dynamic theological method can be further refined to express the idea that the centre of Christian belief is both to change the world to better conform to the purposes of the Creator God and to recognize that we are all called to be makers of history, to perceive all life's possibilities and to recognize our potential to assume the full stature of the divine.

To summarize some of the concerns of this section, I refer to the definition of black theology (which conforms more to the second method of doing theology discussed above) given at the 'Challenging Racism in Britain' consultation of 1 November 1987. The Consultation produced what was called The All Saints Declaration, which observed of black theology that it affirms black people as persons of worth and dignity, created in the image of God; that it reveals in the lives of black people the hidden mystery of a God who, through Jesus Christ, is healing and redeeming; that as a praxis it is a motivation for reflection and action which prophetically challenges and transforms society and which provides an impetus for solidarity among and between all oppressed peoples.[4]

PROBLEMS WITH THE DESIGNATION 'BLACK'

I pause here to consider the meaning of the term 'black'. In the face of the diversity of national origin, language and colour to be found among black people, it should not surprise one to note that the term 'black' has no universal acceptance even among black people. There are some who are reluctant to use it as a form of self-definition because of its negative connotations. In Britain especially there are still some old-style West Indians who are content to be called 'Coloureds'. Among Asian people, to be willing to be called black seems a denial of their cultural particularity and uniqueness. What describes them, they would argue, is their Asian culture. They fear being submerged into a culture of blackness which they understand as West Indian. The unstated anxiety, I suspect, is that identification with West Indians is identification with a further form of inferiority. In some black professional associations, for example those comprising lawyers and probation officers, Asians have hived themselves off and formed Indian associations. It therefore appears that even in the face of a common experience of discrimination and inequality blackness has not afforded black people sufficient cohesion to make common cause against the injustice caused by racism.

In the light of such resistance to the 'black' designation, therefore, any working definition we devise must be broad and inclusive. It must bring within the ambit of common action those who acknowledge that they are bound together by common experience. In South Africa the Black Consciousness Movement defined blackness as 'an attitude of the mind; a way of life'. There is, therefore, a voluntary principle that allows one to make a choice to be part of the common struggle for justice. However, it is not always the case that such choices fulfil what we believe about ourselves. In a racist society one's colour (whatever shade of black) invites racist notions. There is nothing one can do about it.

THE BLACK IDENTITY

There are, however, two identifiable commonalities among black people in Britain today: *history* and *experience*.

The black presence in Britain is the historical product of the British colonial and imperialist exploits. British people ventured into the then unknown world to amass wealth and power. As she extended her realm and influence, Britain spread her culture, values and institutions.

For the Afro-Caribbean blacks the experience of slavery has had deep-seated psychological consequences: a people bought and sold like economic commodities, transmigrated in an often violent and dehumanizing manner, can never outlive the deep scars which experience has caused. This subjection of black people was justified on the grounds that black people were considered to be a savage people, less than human. James Anthony Froude expressed the mood of his day when he wrote, following a visit to the West Indies: 'The poor Black was a faithful servant as long as he was a slave. As freeman he is conscious of his inferiority at the bottom of his heart . . . We have a population to deal with, the enormous majority of whom are of an inferior race. . .'[5]

It is a measure of the resilience of the early slaves that they treasured their human dignity, built their community, resisted and rebelled against the violence of the slave-owners and culture of the master.

There then developed among them a distillation of social and religious values which was an amalgam of, on the one hand, practices vaguely remembered from their time of freedom back in Africa which were maintained through association with other African cultural beliefs and, on the other hand, the religion and culture of their slave-masters. Thereby was shaped a new and unique community which sustained black people through horrendous experiences.

The dialectic between the beliefs, practices and culture of the home country and the adopted country is mirrored in the tension between resistance and acceptance that one sees in black immigrants from Asia and Africa: resistance to wholesale subjugation of social organization and the undermining of the cultural/religious values; acceptance of the promise of justice and democratic systems as well as the moral values which enhanced indigenous life.

This bifocal view of the encounter with the early settlers is illustrated in the novel *Things Fall Apart* by the Nigerian novelist Chinua Achebe. In it he explores the view that the success of the missionary venture in Africa was both a judgement on the bankruptcy of some of the prevailing African traditional customs which were ripe for change as well as an illustration of the attraction of a religion based on the God of Justice. He refers to a would-be convert, Nwoye, who goes against the logic of the elders and against customs to embrace this new religion: 'It was not the cold logic of the Trinity that captivated him . . . It was something felt in the marrow. The hymn about the brother who sat in darkness and fear seemed to answer a vague and persistent question that haunted his soul.'[6] Drawing from the history of the Caribbean, the South African author Peter Abrahams refers to just this quality of tenacity and will in order to explain why it is that black people have never totally adapted to the ways of the white man. Referring to a family of slaves plotting an escape, he captures one ruminating: 'To do nothing is wrong. To do nothing is to be part of the thing they do to us; to be part of the destruction of our people. And that the ancestors will not forgive.'[7]

Besides their common experience under British white supremacy, black people came to this country fired with perhaps sentimental beliefs about British virtues of fairness and justice. Yet they found rejection and hostility in the home of Western Christian civilization. Peter Fryer documents how by intrigue and subterfuge successive governments sought to restrict – and even hoped to reverse – immigration from black countries. Racism became enshrined in law when the Commonwealth Immigrants Act of 1962 was passed. Then a British passport no longer allowed unrestricted enjoyment of the rights of a citizen. In effect, the Act made black people second-class citizens. From then to the present there has developed the myth that black people are 'the problem', rather than the evils of social inequality, deprivation and lack of access to the economic well-being so essential for human dignity.[8]

The syndrome of an alien minority suffering isolation and working hard to better themselves against the odds is firmly ingrained in the psyche of black people in Britain, especially in the early immigrants. And so they tend to be suspicious of the power or class élite, to defer to those in authority and to avoid political confrontation until one has no other option but to defend oneself or one's interests.

It soon became evident that far from having their hopes of self-betterment realized, black immigrants had to live with poverty and suffer homelessness or rent overcrowded, overpriced and dilapidated dwellings. Through racism, they were for a long time prevented from putting their names on council housing lists or entering the property market. As soon as the economic recession began to bite, they were the targets of popular hate. Where they were competing for the kind of jobs that hitherto whites had disdained, they were now the objects of violence and intimidation in the workplace. For black people that is and has been the universal experience. Their dreams were shattered and the crisis of confidence brought alienation and often despair.

RACISM AND NATIONALITY

The sum total of racial disadvantage caused by prejudice and fortified by the ability to exploit and exclude black people from resources and from effective decision-making because of the colour of their skin, equals racism. But it must be remembered that in Britain racism is a sub-class within the overall structural inequality caused by class stratification. Class differentiation, together with its attendant privileges and social esteem for those at the top, is at the heart of British social organization. It is therefore not surprising that racism is so endemic in Britain.

Racism entails, at one level, a confusion about nationality and, at another, various confused perceptions about the nature of nationalism which in Britain serve to fuel racial intolerance. There is a prevailing tendency to speak about black people wholly as if they were immigrants or aliens. To wear a black skin confirms that one does not belong. The truth is, of course, that more and more black people are British by birth, loyalty and commitment. What distinguishes them from white British people, besides the colour of their skin, is that their ideas and culture convey a language and way of life rooted in Africa or the West Indies. Yet there is in British society a strong reluctance to accept the cultural diversity that this entails – an emerging British culture that is affected by the customs of the wider Commonwealth peoples. In the frontline of the urban uprisings of recent years are black British youth who will not trade off their Britishness and yet will not be assimilated into a stagnant British culture. However, hostility and rejection are part of their daily experience in their dealings especially with the police; and they meet with mistrust on the dole queue and suspicions from their white neighbours. Yet many black people have been making a contribution to the sporting, musical, political, religious, intellectual and business traditions of this country for a very long time. They pay taxes, they go to war; as Peter Fryer notes, 'Black people born in Britain are a permanent part of British society.'[9]

However, black people in Britain do not simply have to cope with the burden of having to prove their belonging by assimilating British values; voices have been raised which suggest that it is logically impossible for black people to acquire British nationality. Enoch Powell argues that black people are 'unassimilable and unassimilated populations . . . alien weeds in the heartland of the state'.[10] He has the support of Sir Alfred Sherman, a former adviser to the British Prime Minister, who invited the French racist politician Jean Marie Le Pen to the Conservative Party Conference in 1987. Sherman asserts that it is impossible to acquire British nationality by mere legislative fiat; 'a passport or residence does not implant national values or patriotism,' he argues.

Of course, the fundamental flaw in these arguments is the assumption that a precondition of being a national of another country is to become totally assimilated into its values and lifestyles and culture. Furthermore, implicit in these views is the notion that a white skin conveys a kind of assimilability that makes it possible for white aliens to become British citizens. Enoch Powell and those of his ilk need to be reminded that nationhood is a dynamic process and is not solely dependent upon one's ability to trace one's roots to an ancestry long past. If that is the case, then there can be *no* purely 'British' citizens, since there is a diversity among the constituents of British society: English, Scot, Irish, Welsh, Cornish, etc. Besides, a large number of leading British personalities came into Britain as refugees or immigrants, many as recently as the end of the Second World War.

Of course, the truth is that British nationality is less culture-determined than it is constituted by a common bond of loyalty to the Crown. That was what a British passport meant and, traditionally, it was not even geographically circumscribed. Besides, cultural diversity is not inimical to the concept of nationhood. The United States of

America has grown out of an acceptance of diversity and is enriched thereby.

The Commonwealth is an expression of such a diversity on a grand scale. It therefore must not be surprising that great diversity is represented in British national life. A tangible example of that diversity is the presence of Japanese Buddhist Peace Pagodas in London and elsewhere. These are a measure of the Japanese cultural incursion that has come with the advent of the Nissan factory and the earlier influx of electronic goods and components.

All nations require injections of cultural dynamism from other lands, and these can be creative and enriching experiences. Society – and *a fortiori* a nation – is a self-creating entity: it can never be fossilized. Rejecting calls for the repatriation of black people (which calls have since died down), the Archbishop of Canterbury, Dr Robert Runcie, said in a lecture to the Birmingham Council for Community Relations in 1982:

> Any talk of repatriating people who have sometimes lived here for more than two generations or who are no longer welcome in their own countries of origin is a dangerous fantasy. We are in fact a multiracial society, and the choice we have is between working to make this fact a matter of pride and celebration, or drifting into a situation where this fact is a matter of lament and despair.[11]

FAITH IN THE CITY

In the light of the above social analysis, we can turn to *Faith in the City*, the 1985 report of the Archbishop's Commission on Urban Priority Areas. Here the concerns of the black community receive understanding and the problems of poverty are firmly addressed. As the commissioners went among inner-city communities they bemoaned the evidence of a divided Britain. It is the poor and deprived who speak through the pages of the Report. The commissioners listened and saw for themselves. The Report restates the fundamental Christian values of social responsibility. It proposes a sharing and a wider distribution of resources and a redressing of the balance of power and opportunity to give the poor and the deprived an even chance.

Significantly, however, the Report fails to address the question of nationality, nor does it face up to the essential or structural inequality in British society. A question that needed to be asked is: How can the structures of Church and society so change as to be more fully representative of contemporary British life? The report is Eurocentric in its mould. No effort is made to examine the history and culture of the black communities. The tone is one of benevolence towards the deprived. It appeals to the conscience of the wealthy and powerful to give due regard to the needs of the poor, the implication being that *they* hold the key to change towards a more just and caring society.

It is not surprising, therefore, that the Report's theological stance articulates what may be termed 'Christendom values': an assertion of Christian values and triumphalism. But there must be a revision of the theological outlook that has for so long undergirded British church and social life. The Church's theological frames of reference, language and world-views, styles of leadership and organization need to be tempered if it is to identify fully with and help black people develop a sense of belonging to it. Belonging presupposes a freedom to make one's contribution to the life of the Church in such a way that change may be discernible. Black people need to own the Church and exercise their freedom within it.

A major defect of the Report is its inadequate and potentially misleading exposition of the nature and task of the Church. One can so easily take away from it the impression that the Church in the inner city is a social welfare or employment agency. Granted, the Church can become the focus of community life and endeavour, but it can hardly possess resources sufficient to accomplish the necessary inner-city regeneration. That is and must be the task of government. There is a further danger, that the Church might be associated too closely with the various government agencies and initiatives such as the Social Services departments and the Manpower Services Commission employment schemes to the extent that the faults within the system could become attributable to the Church.

The Church can hardly be accountable for resources which it does not ultimately control. However, even if the Churches were to set up their own schemes, the energy required to find adequate resources and manage them would be disproportionate to the time and energy needed to tackle deprivation. Allegedly poor people will need to find large sums of money, negotiate with government agencies or industry or local authorities and be adept at operating through a maze of bureaucracies. And yet such initiatives, especially if they lead to enterprise and accomplishment, could boost community life remarkably.

The concept so beloved of the Victorian Catholic Renewal movement, that the Church of God stands at the centre of human deprivation to proclaim the glory of God, urgently needs revision. We need to draw attention to the Church built not of walls but of people; we need to identify with the people whom we serve and so empower them that they may more fully take control of their lives. I am referring to the biblical idea of 'the ark of God' which dwelt among God's people and with whom God tasted both victory and defeat. The Church is accordingly a sign of the immanence of God. Communities dwelt in by God are spiritually privileged. At the heart of the community, God shares in the struggles and the hopes of his people.

This model of the Church raises theological possibilities for pastoral care – possibilities which I have always believed are the privilege of the Church of England. A significant one is that of an interaction between the Church (as the gathered ecclesial and eucharistic or charismatic community) and the wider community which it seeks to serve, such that the people of faith are indistinguishable from their community save in the deeper spiritual understanding of witness and service which undergirds their participation in community. Prayer, worship and action would then become part of the activity of the community. This ties in with Philip Berryman's judgement – in the context of a discussion of the development of basic ecclesial communities – that a community emerges only when people 'understand their life in the light of God's Word, and form among themselves bonds of support and experience [the] unity that is the germ of a future united community'.[12]

The call to community is a call to neighbourliness. Community is emphatically not merely the aggregate of individuals who make up the whole, despite Margaret Thatcher's philosophy that 'there are no communities, only individuals'. In fact this ideology of individualism serves only to undermine *koinonia* and interdependence.

Finally, I want to make a passing reference to renewal: a need for change. As the Church, we should resist the temptation to model ourselves along the lines of the prevailing social norms and traditions. A living Church is one which is conscious of its need to be renewed; a society in search of truth and justice must be prepared to change. The Creator God accomplishes his purposes because he has been ready to change so that creation can be made perfect. One understands only too well that there is a certain amount of cosiness, charm and security under the cover of tradition and unchanging norms and values. But that is a denial of the incarnation: 'The Word became flesh and dwelt among us' (John 1.14). Out of the activity of God's people we see a vision of the struggles which will bring blessings. Kenneth Leech, in a Jubilee Lecture, 'The Resurrection of the Christian Social Voice' (1976), has this to say: 'We have lost the hope of renewal, of a new order, the Kingdom of justice, love and peace.' He goes on to make reference to what could be described as the spiritual liberative programme of local parishes so that they become i) centres for deepening the inner life; ii) centres for local community action and caring and iii) campaigning centres for righteousness and peace, so that all individual caring is set firmly in the context of the Kingdom of God and his righteousness.[13]

Rudolf J. Siebert aptly summarizes our concerns in this section: 'Only the reconciled society is a free society and only a free society is reconciled.'[14]

THEOLOGICAL IMPLICATIONS

How does all this impinge on the theological practices of black people in Britain? How does the black experience inform theological understanding and theology affect the black people's action for justice? And what is so distinctive, in any case, about the theology done from a black perspective?

In this section I want to look at five areas which involve an appreciation of the contribution of black Christians to the theological task. But I would like to preface my remarks with the following three observations:

1 Black religious practice in Britain has a common thread that runs through all denominations.
2 Racial discrimination in Britain has imposed a common objective on black people as a group to work together for racial justice, and indeed this is the only basis on which they will overcome.
3 The black theology of liberation expresses the deepest yearnings of the black people of faith in Britain, affirms black personality and nourishes their hopes.

Black spirituality and community

Any understanding of the spirituality of black people has got to begin with community.

Community is the substance of life and belonging. The people of God are an expression of God's community with his people. As among the ancient Israelites, community breaks down through sin and selfishness, and when it breaks down God deserts his people and they become prey to the ravenous wolves.

But community is also a means of self-realization when, in the African idiom, we are who we are because of others. A community expresses the common will, realizes and dispenses the common wealth. Out of it life's values are sustained and through it common tasks are accomplished.

A community is an organizational unit that devises common strategies, promotes dialogue within and, externally, with institutional forces and engages in action for change and mutual fulfilment. Paul Gilroy quotes with approval one Mellucci, who identifies the spiritual component as one which connects the diverse social and political movements. 'Spirituality', he writes, 'has acquired powerful radical dimensions not only because religious language can express the intensity of aspirations for which no secular alternative is available but because the political order which these movements criticise and oppose is itself increasingly secular in its rationalisations.'[15] Such a vew of community is considered part of the natural order in the black world and needs no justification, whereas the Western philosophical mindset perceives a dichotomy between the sacred and the secular. The coherence and homogeneity of all creation with all humanity explains why community is considered holy and nature sacred in many traditional religions.

The pilgrim experience

British blacks share together the *pilgrim* experience. It must have taken the faith of Abraham for many to travel to unknown lands. They all come from places far away to claim a sense of belonging in this land where God will help them to take root (Gen. 12.1–3), and they bring blessings to their adopted country.

Black people have a right to claim Abraham the wandering Aramaean as their ancestor. If they do so, then they are assured of the privilege of seeing the day of the coming of Christ and rejoicing (cf. John 8.56). But, for a Christian, there is also the consciousness that this is no final resting place, and so the pilgrim fathers dwell in tents or tabernacle, getting themselves ready for the call of God. Meanwhile there are blessings to be bestowed, the household of faith to be built and the world to be made more perfect.

The fate of the cities which reject God's messengers is stated in Luke 10.10–12. And so we are called to proclaim judgement – 'nevertheless know this, that the kingdom of God has come near' (v. 11). Black people live through the crisis of faith, in the tension of seeking fulfilment even within the society that they believe is under judgement. They are on the frontiers, straddling the divide between those who make a positive affirmation of faith and others who, while unable to make a faith testimony, yet share identifiable concerns about justice.

Blacks can lead the way towards radical ways of collaborative activity. They can identify with an impotent and weeping God of the ghetto, one who suffers crucifixion each time black humanity is insulted. He shares their powerlessness in the face of human complicity in evil. And yet out of their belief in that God, they can rejoice that they are 'no longer aliens in a foreign land, but fellow-citizens with God's people, members of God's household' (Eph. 2.19, NEB).

Liberation theology concerns

Next I turn to that cluster of issues relating to *justice, liberation* and *peace*. Indeed a great deal of black theology and liberation theology has concentrated so much on these matters that I must simply draw out pointers. Yet, in the British context and arising from my South African experience, I do not want to trivialize the significance of liberation.

I do not want to suggest that the British democratic institutions are without integrity or that they absolutely block access for blacks and that it is necessary to seek to break them up. It is only in those matters relating to the denial of nationality or citizenship that I would hazard to make reference to liberation. And yet it can be argued both that the incidence of police brutality has reached such proportions that black people can no longer identify with the State which they represent and that immigration policies are such that they can be considered repressive. And so we have recourse to the Jubilee proclamation in Isaiah 61 and Luke 4, and the liberation theme in Exodus: 'I have seen the affliction of my people who are in Egypt, and have heard their cry . . . I know their sufferings, and I have come down to deliver them' (Exod. 3:7–8).

The link between Exodus and Jubilee is precisely in the fact that the God who frees his people from external domination will not countenance the assumption of practices within the liberated Israelite community that are contrary to the principles of justice and cause God to act to liberate them. But, more importantly, liberation–justice is about the restoration of community; about 'shalom'; about just and peaceable relations; about harmony. Justice is an obligation of all societies, because to practise injustice is to deny one's own freedom.

Following the disturbances in Handsworth in September 1985, the Handsworth Forum, an association of clergy based in Handsworth, issued this statement: 'God has given us a vision and a task. The vision is of a society where, under God, everyone has equal value, and where justice and peace are seen to prevail over the forces of oppression and destruction. The task is to work together with God towards that end by all just means.'[16] We have the capacity to work towards that vision because we can see that it is an achievable goal. That is hope. As we progress the struggle for liberation and justice, we celebrate now all manner of victories: the victory of Christian conviction, the victory of hope, the victory of love and the will to persevere. And so, in the words of the South African theologian Dr John de Gruchy, we are urged to rejoice in the Lord always: 'So our little or large penultimate, proximate victories, those moments when justice is done and reconciliation becomes a reality, become pointers to the ultimate judgment and redemption of God.'[17]

Theologizing in the black mode

We need to adopt a healthy scepticism about the claims of ownership of theology. We need to develop a theological model that has intellectual rigour and yet is earthed in the reality of black life and experience. That can best be done by taking the disciplines of the humanities seriously and by drawing from the consensus of faith and wisdom embedded in black culture.

The history of black peoples, their culture and philosophy of life, do not all deserve to be thrown overboard but need to be nurtured and reinterpreted with conceptual tools that affirm the black experience. Therefore we should affirm the narrative model of biblical interpretation, which is a return to the primacy of the oral tradition that is in danger of being lost. Likewise, spontaneity in song and dance, as well as the absence of inhibitions, needs to be revived again. Note how David 'danced before the Lord with all his might', brushing aside the embarrassment of his wife Michal (2 Sam. 6.14, 21–2).

Black Christianity in Britain has grown into an understanding of its true self, especially in culture and worship. Gilroy explains the effect of this phenomenon in these terms: 'Affection and intimacy are created in collective rituals, and a view of society which stresses its "ontological depth", demanding specific standards of truth from the forms of knowledge which will guide the community towards authentic freedom in the future'.[18] We have begun to see representatives of black worship in the media – for example, gospel music has become very popular – and the annual West Indian carnivals in Notting Hill and Handsworth express black personality. But deep down these manifestations of black culture are also a politico-religious testament to the pain and aspirations of black people. Precisely because of that, black music, dance, poetry and other forms of creative cultural expression are legitimate vehicles of black theology.

Black theology and the white-led Churches

Finally, all this has some implications for those who practise their religion within such an ethos of alienation. Black theology essentially relates to black people. It is the black person's tool for affirmation of personhood and understanding of God's activity. It can function with credibility in the hands of blacks, but white people too will need tools of interpretation to unravel its meaning and significance. I therefore take the view that black people must themselves take charge of the business of religious affirmation from their context.

However, black people live with the reality of the dominance of white society. For many black people black theology will be exercised within the white-led Churches. In that case it can become a means of mutual misunderstanding. White people need to understand the religious dimension of black life in its authentic and primal sense. In that sense it can mark a contribution to race relations. But much more than that, this understanding should lead to the formation of alliances for justice across the colour spectrum – what in the United States has come to be known as the 'Rainbow Coalition' associated with the presidential candidacy of the Revd Jesse Jackson.

One can therefore envisage a revised system of training for ministry. Black people will lay the foundations for their participation in the Church by undertaking a programme of learning that explores their deeper being in order to offer the experience of faith of the black Christians to the wider Church. Only fully liberated people can freely participate and contribute to Church and society.

In order to open up black culture and share its riches with the community Gayraud Wilmore suggests that we have to call for the tools of interpretation vested in the black experience, culture and systems of knowledge, which reveal that the God of history has been at work in black communities for many hundreds of years.[19] The paradigmatic shift required here will give a more authentic statement of black understandings of God and how the vision of a just and reconciled society flows from such a vision.

Notes

I am indebted to many friends and colleagues who read and made comments on the original script. Special thanks go to the Black Christian Studies Seminar at the Queen's College, Birmingham, and the College Seminar at Ripon College, Cuddesdon, where versions of this paper were read.

1 Referred to in P. Fryer, 'The History of English Racism, Part 2', *Ethical Record* 93.4 (April 1988), pp. 18ff.
2 J. H. Cone, *Black Theology and Black Power* (New York, Seabury Press, 1969), p. 31.
3 B. Lonergan, *Method in Theology* (Darton, Longman & Todd, 1975), p. 23.
4 The Community and Race Relations Unit, *The All Saints Declaration* (British Council of Churches, 1987).
5 Quoted in Fryer, 'The History of English Racism, Part 2', p. 18.
6 C. Achebe, *Things Fall Apart* (Heinemann, 1958), p. 134.
7 P. Abrahams, *The View From Mount Coyabe* (Faber & Faber, 1985), p. 15.
8 See J. S. Gundara, 'Racism and the National Question', a paper presented at the New Expressions of Racism in Europe workshop, Amsterdam, October 1987, obtainable from International Alert, London.

9 Fryer, 'The History of English Racism, Part 2', p. 22.
10 P. Gilroy, *There Ain't No Black in the Union Jack* (Hutchinson, 1987), p. 59.
11 'Racial Attitudes in Britain – The Way Forward' published by the Church Information Office, London, 2 July 1982.
12 P. Berryman, *The Religious Roots of Rebellion* (SCM Press, 1984), p. 334.
13 K. Leech, 'The Resurrection of the Catholic Social Voice', *Theology* 77 (1974), p. 654.
14 R. J. Siebert, 'Jacob and Jesus: Recent Marxist Readings of the Bible' in N. K. Gottwald (ed.), *The Bible and Liberation* (New York, Orbis Books, 1984), p. 501.
15 Gilroy, op. cit., p. 227.
16 Unpublished statement issued by the Handsworth Forum, September 1985.
17 J. de Gruchy, 'The Struggle for Justice and Ministry of Reconciliation', *South African Journal of Theology* 62 (1988), p. 52.
18 Gilroy, op.cit., p. 218.
19 G. Wilmore, *Black Religion and Black Radicalism* (New York, Seabury Press, 1980).

6
Faith in the City:
A Jewish Response

Dan Cohn-Sherbok

THE CHIEF RABBI'S RESPONSE TO *FAITH IN THE CITY*

Faith in the City has evoked considerable reaction from various quarters of society – it has even touched a sensitive nerve in the Jewish community. In an article in the *Jewish Chronicle*,[1] the Chief Rabbi, Lord Jakobovits, criticized its findings at several points and offered a Jewish alternative for combating the hardships of inner-city life.

The experience of the Jewish community, he argues, can serve as a model for those who are deprived in modern society. According to the Chief Rabbi, it was not by preaching Jewish power or non-violence that Jews were able to break out of the ghettos. Rather it was through ambition, education, and hard work. But is such a policy of self-help the only response that the Jewish community can make to the Report? The purpose of this study is to present an alternative view – to find within the Jewish tradition spiritual resources which reinforce the Report's commitment to empathize with the suffering of those who are poor and oppressed and to side with them in their struggle for a better life.

In his reponse to *Faith in the City*, the Chief Rabbi emphasizes that Judaism is in complete agreement with the basic assumption underlying the study, namely that religious leaders and organizations should address themselves to important social problems. In this regard he notes that the biblical prophets were history's supreme leaders of opposition. Yet for the Chief Rabbi there are important reasons why Jews are unable to accept many of the conclusions of the Report.

First, the historical experience of Jewry has been entirely different from that of Christians. Until very recent times Jews have been a small minority, subject to discrimination and persecution. For centuries Jews were forced to live in crowded ghettos in the most adverse conditions. Yet such experience, Lord Jakobovits argues, should provide instructive lessons for those presently enduring similar circumstances. Quoting from a farewell speech he gave in America in the 1960s, he offers advice to today's black community:

> How did we break out of our ghettos and enter the mainstream of society and its privileges? . . . We worked on ourselves, not on others. We gave a

better education to our children than anybody else had. We hallowed our home life. We channelled the ambition of our youngsters to academic excellence . . . we rooted out crime and indolence from our midst, by making every Jew feel responsible for the fate of all Jews.

On the basis of such experience, the Chief Rabbi prescribes a similar course of action for blacks who suffer similar disabilities in the modern world:

Let them give two or three hours' extra schooling every day to their children, as we gave to ours; let them build up by charitable endeavours great federations of social welfare, as we did for our poor; let them instil in all negroes a feeling of shame for any crime committed by a negro . . . let them encourage ambition and excellence in every negro child, as Jewish parents encouraged in their children – and they will pull down their ghetto walls as surely as we demolished ours.

In connection with this policy of self-improvement, Lord Jakobovits points out that though the Jewish community was anxious to preserve its own identity, British Jews never demanded that British society ought to change its character and assume a new multi-ethnic form. There was never a demand that there be public allowance for varying ethnic traditions, whether in policing policies or in family counselling under local authority auspices. 'We were quite content', he writes, 'for Britain to remain "ethnocentrically" British.' Jews thus did not insist on public help, nor on changes in official policies; instead the Jewish community created its own educational and social institutions designed to preserve and transmit the Jewish heritage in a contemporary context. Such social objectives took time to attain; it was only after several generations that Jews were able to integrate fully into British society. Agitation and social unrest were never considered the proper course of action. From such an experience it may be salutary, the Chief Rabbi states, to remind those presently enduring much hardship and despair that others have faced similar trials before them, and that self-reliant efforts and perseverance eventually pay off, turning humiliation into dignity and depression into hope and fulfilment.

The Chief Rabbi continues his defence of self-help by illustrating that such a policy is based on Jewish religious teaching which extols the virtues of work. The Jewish work ethic, he declares, is positive and demanding. Human history begins with God's command to Adam in the Garden of Eden 'to till it and keep it' (Gen. 2.15). According to the Talmud, no work is too menial to compromise human dignity and self-respect. The path to true contentment is through diligent work, as the psalmist declared: 'You shall eat the fruit of the labour of your hands; you shall be happy, and it shall be well with you' (Ps. 128.2).

Conversely, idleness is viewed in the Jewish tradition as a waste of human resources. Furthermore, Judaism does not frown on gaining wealth, nor does it demand that wealth should be shared or distributed to equalize rich and poor. On the contrary, riches (assuming they are honestly accumulated) are seen as a sign of divine grace to be enjoyed in moderation.

According to the Chief Rabbi the operative words in the Jewish vocabulary concerning relief for the poor are neither entitlement nor compensation. When the Bible demands of the haves to stretch out a helping arm to the have-nots (using the words 'you shall open your hand', Deut. 15.8), the 'open hand' is not the beggar's asserting his entitlement to receive, but the giver's acknowledging his duty not to be tight-fisted. When the concept of compensation appears in the Jewish tradition, it has a specialized meaning. The Talmud states that 'more than the wealthy man gives to the poor, the poor gives to the wealthy'. The poor man ennobles the giver and is compensated by the knowledge that he gives more than he receives; the rich man is compensated for the diminution of his wealth knowing that he has gained more than he has lost. Here is found the Jewish solution to the problem of humiliation felt by those who are impoverished. Self-respect derives from a feeling that one is contributing to the needs of others. Jewish law therefore stipulates that even the poor man is required to donate some of his proceeds from charity for the relief of others. 'There is a double benefit in this,' the Chief Rabbi writes:

> Even the deprived person must learn to part with some of what he receives, thus training him in the art and satisfaction of giving; and his dignity is to be restored by letting him experience a sense of equality with the rich in supporting others in need. In this connection, Judaism defines the highest kind of charity as a form of self-help – the giver is to assist the poor man to rehabilitate himself by lending him money, taking him into partnership, employing him, or giving him work.

In the light of such theological views, as well as the Jewish experience, the Chief Rabbi concludes that Judaism pre-eminently urges the building up of self-respect by encouraging ambition and enterprise through a work ethic designed to eliminate idleness and to nurture pride in human labour. Though Lord Jakobovits believes that the affluent section of society should provide more social agencies and counselling services and capital for prudent enterprises in the inner cities, he notes that these areas are now denuded of Jewish communities. Thus they have neither the Jewish spiritual nor social workers which would be required to operate such projects, nor the smaller assets under Jewish religious control which would be required.

But even more important for the recovery of the health of the inner cities than such a programme is the repair of home life as the bastion of love, care, decency and every social virtue. In a Jewish blueprint for the regeneration of the inner cities, the Chief Rabbi maintains that the family would feature prominently:

> For when the family breaks down, the most essential conditions for raising happy, law abiding and creatively ambitious citizens are frustrated . . . Through a dedication to hard work, self-help, and the rebuilding of family life, the new ghettos can be transformed as were the old, and the resources of the nation can be shared by all.

There is no doubt the Chief Rabbi's description of self-help in the Jewish community is correct; for centuries Jews have been able to free themselves from disabilities through hard work and dedication. Further, there are ample sources within the biblical and rabbinic tradition to support his contention that the Jewish faith extols work and cherishes family life. Nevertheless, these themes do not exhaust Jewish teaching about religion and society – the Jewish heritage is rich in resources which deal directly with social deprivation. By focusing simply on those aspects of the Jewish heritage which support his vision of labour and family life, the Chief Rabbi has given too narrow a vision of social concern within the Jewish faith. What is required instead is a more comprehensive account of Jewish social ethics than that given by Lord Jakobovits in his response to *Faith in the City*.

THE EXODUS EXPERIENCE

For the Jewish people, social concern grows out of the experiences of their ancestors in Egypt. There the Jewish people were exploited and oppressed: the Egyptians overwhelmed the Hebrew slaves with work; they 'made their lives bitter with hard service, in mortar and brick, and in all kinds of work in the field' (Exod. 1.14). Such affliction caused the people to cry out to God for liberation, and in response God decreed: 'I have seen the affliction of my people who are in Egypt, and have heard their cry because of their taskmasters; I know their sufferings, and I have come down to deliver them out of the hand of the Egyptians' (Exod. 3.7–8).

To the Jewish mind the Exodus was a pivotal event in the history of the nation – it is the salvation experience *par excellence*. In the unfolding of the divine plan of deliverance, God revealed himself through Moses, and nowhere is this act of liberation celebrated more than in the festival of Passover. The Passover Seder envisages the Exodus experience as a symbol of freedom from oppression, and the

117

whole of the Haggadah is pervaded by the image of God as the Saviour of mankind. For this reason, the Passover service begins with an ancient formulaic invitation to those who hunger or are in need to participate in the festival: 'This is the bread of affliction that our fathers ate in the Land of Egypt. All who hunger, let them come and eat: all who are in need, let them come and celebrate the Passover. Now we are here – next year we shall be free men.' Any Jew who sits down to the Passover meal and is oblivious of the call of those who are in want has missed the meaning of the celebration.

During the service the leader displays the unleavened bread to stimulate the curiosity of youngsters at the meal. It is then the turn of the youngest child to ask about the nature of the Passover festivities – the entire ritual of the Seder hinges on these inquiries. In reply the leader recites the narrative of the Exodus, stressing the themes of liberation and freedom from oppression:

> We were Pharaoh's slaves in Egypt; and the Lord our God brought us out thereof with a mighty hand and an outstretched arm. Now, had not the Holy One brought out our fathers from Egypt, then we and our children and our children's children would be enslaved to Pharaoh in Egypt. Wherefore, even were we all wise men, all men of understanding, all advanced in years, all men with knowledge of the Torah, it would yet be our duty to recount the story of the coming forth from Egypt; and all who recount at length the story of the coming forth from Egypt are verily to be praised.[2]

This response implies that the Passover does not simply commemorate a triumph of remote antiquity. Rather, the Passover ceremony is a celebration of the emancipation of each Jew in every generation, for had it not been for the Exodus Jews would still be slaves in Egypt. Historical continuity is at the heart of this understanding, and is illustrated further by the response made to the wicked son who asks, 'What mean ye by this service?' In response the leader states:

> He infers 'ye'; not himself. By shutting himself off from the general body, it is as though he denies the existence of God. Therefore thou shouldst distress him too, replying: 'This is done because of that which the Lord did unto me when I came forth out of Egypt' – Unto me, not him; for if he had been there he would not have been delivered.

The keynote of the Haggadah is enshrined in a central pledge of the Seder: 'It is this Divine pledge that hath stood by our fathers and by us also. Not only one man hath risen against us to destroy us, but in every generation men have risen against us to destroy us: But the Holy One delivereth us always from their hand.' Here Pharaoh's action is seen as a paradigm of all attempts by Israel's enemies to persecute the Jewish people. Echoes of centuries of persecution are evoked by these words, yet it is made clear that God has been, and will continue to be, on the side of his oppressed people. In the symbols of the Passover meal, such deliverance is re-enacted. Explaining this symbolism the leader states with regard to the shank-bone:

> The Passover Lamb that our fathers used to eat when the Temple was still standing – what is the reason? It is because the Holy One, Blessed be He, passed over the house of our fathers in Egypt, as it is said; 'Ye shall say, It is the sacrifice of the Lord's Passover, who passed over the houses of the children of Israel in Egypt, when He smote the Egyptians and delivered our houses. And the people bowed the head and worshipped.'

The unleavened bread is the bread of affliction, the historical emblem of the Exodus. The leader declares that it is the symbol of sympathy for the enslaved as well as of freedom from oppression:

> This unleavened bread that we eat – what is the reason? It is because there was no time for our ancestors' dough to become leavened, before the King, King of all Kings, the Holy One, revealed Himself to them and redeemed them, as it is said: 'And they baked unleavened cakes of the dough which they brought forth out of Egypt, for it was not leavened: because they were thrust out of Egypt, and could not tarry, neither had they prepared for themselves any victual.'

The bitter herbs are the symbol of bitterness and servitude which serves as a reminder to the Jew that it is his duty as a descendant of slaves to lighten the stranger's burden:

> This bitter herb that we eat – what is its reason? It is because the Egyptians embittered the life of our ancestors in Egypt, as it is said: 'And they made their lives bitter with hard bondage, in mortar and brick, and in all manner of service in the field, all their service, when they made them serve, was with rigour.'

The lesson of the Passover service – deeply engraved on the hearts of the Jewish nation – is that persecution and divine deliverance are realities of the present as well as the past. In each generation, Jews must think of themselves as delivered from a perpetual enemy and should assume the responsibility of rescuing those who suffer under oppression. 'In each and every generation,' the Haggadah states,

> it is a man's duty to regard himself as though he went forth out of Egypt, as it is said, 'And thou shalt tell thy son in that day saying, "This is done because of that which the Lord did unto me when I came forth out of Egypt." Not our fathers only did the Holy One redeem, but us too. He redeemed them, as it is said, "And He brought us out from thence, that He might bring us in, to give us the Land which He swore unto our fathers."'

119

The Passover celebration is thus a symbolic exaltation of freedom; each Jew is to rejoice in God's liberation of his ancestors in which he has taken part. Throughout the history of the Jewish people this festival has awakened the spirit of the people to the significance of human liberation.

This Jewish understanding of the Exodus event has much in common with contemporary liberation theology, which has influenced much of the theological reflection contained in *Faith in the City*. Like liberation theologians, the Jews have found renewed strength and hope in the message of the Exodus. The Passover ceremony unites the Jewish people with their ancestors who endured slavery and oppression in Egyptian bondage. Despite the persecution of centuries, the Jewish nation is confident of eventual deliverance and the ultimate redemption of humankind. The message of the Exodus calls the Jewish people to hold steadfast to their conviction that justice and freedom will prevail throughout the world. The Passover, by symbolizing the primal act of liberation, points to a future and ultimate redemption of the human family.

THE PROPHETIC MESSAGE

Another central dimension of biblical theology linked with human liberation and freedom is the message of the prophets. According to Scripture, the role of the prophet was to be the social conscience of the nation. The Hebrew prophets' experience was of a God so concerned with social justice that they perpetually struggled to rescue the nation from its iniquity and draw the people back to the faith of their ancestors. Amos for example – the earliest of the classical Hebrew prophets – inveighed against the people because of oppression, bribery and injustice. Several decades after Amos began his ministry in Israel, Isaiah began his prophetic mission in Judah. God had chosen Israel to produce justice, he proclaimed, but instead she created bloodshed. Like Amos, he protested against the indifference of the rich to the poor and oppressed and he condemned the offering of sacrifice without a concomitant quest for righteousness.

According to Isaiah, Israel is a sinful nation – a band of wrong-doers; the nation has turned away from God. Thus he condemns the women of Jerusalem who arrogantly and wantonly stroll through the streets, the priests and false prophets who drunkenly proclaim their messages, and the judges who issue tyrannical judgements and cheat the poor, widows and orphans so as to grow wealthy on bribes. These classical prophets – as well as other prophets who carried on their message – became the conscience of the nation: they attacked the exploitation of the poor by the rich and the people's iniquity. Their words have echoed down the centuries as a call for justice and righteousness for all people.

THE KINGDOM OF GOD AND RABBINIC ETHICS

For the Jews the prophetic tradition amplified the Exodus experience – God is conceived as demanding compassion, justice and righteousness for all those who suffer under the yoke of oppression and exploitation. This concern for those who endure hardship continued throughout the rabbinic period. According to the rabbis, God is a supreme ruler who calls all men to join him in bringing about the Kingdom of God on earth. This Kingdom consists in the reign of trust, righteousness and holiness among all nations. The fulfilment of this conception ultimately rests with the coming of the Messiah; nevertheless, it is man's duty to participate in the creation of a better world in anticipation of the messianic redemption. In the words of the rabbis: 'Man is a co-worker with God in the work of creation.'

According to rabbinic theology, man is the centre of creation, for it is only he among all created beings who can through righteousness make the Kingdom glorious. In rabbinic midrash, the view is expressed that God's Kingship did not come into question until man was created: 'When the Holy One, blessed be He, consulted the Torah as to the creation of the world, he answered, "Master of the world, if there be no host, over whom will the King reign, and if there be no peoples praising him, where is the glory of the King?"' It is only man, then, who can make the Kingdom glorious: God wants to reign over free agents who can act as his co-partners in perfecting the world. What God requires is obedience to his ways of righteousness and justice: 'You are my lovers and friends. You walk in my ways,' God declares to Israel. 'As the Omnipotent is merciful and gracious, long-suffering and abundant in goodness, so be ye . . . feeding the hungry, giving drink to the thirsty, clothing the naked, ransoming the captives, and marrying the orphans.'

The idea of the Kingdom is conceived by the rabbis as ethical in character. In the words of the distinguished scholar, Solomon Schechter:

> If, then, the Kingdom of God was thus originally intended to be in the midst of men and for men at large (as represented by Adam), if its first preachers were, like Abraham, ex-heathens, who addressed themselves to heathens, if, again, the essence of their preaching was righteousness and justice, and if, lastly, the Kingdom does not mean a hierarchy, but any form of government conducted on the principles of righteousness, holiness,

justice, and charitableness, then we may safely maintain that the Kingdom of God, as taught by Judaism in one of its aspects, is universal in its aims.[3]

According to the Hebrew Scriptures, God's identification with morality is absolute. In the prophetic writings, as we have seen, the primacy of ethical behaviour is asserted, and this emphasis continues throughout rabbinic literature. Believing themselves to possess an authentic oral tradition as to the meaning of Scripture, the rabbis expounded and amplified the biblical ethical injunctions. Thus throughout rabbinic literature the rabbis sought to ensure that God's moral precepts were upheld. In this light the Jewish people are acceptable to God only when they fulfil the commandments of the Torah. Hence we read in the Midrash: 'It is like a King who said to his wife, "Deck yourself with all your ornaments that you may be acceptable to me." So God says to Israel, "Be distinguished by the commandments that you may be acceptable to me." '

For the rabbis, morality and religion form a single whole, inseparable from one another. Faith in God entails the obligation to be good, for God has commanded that his people follow his moral dictates. This view is eloquently illustrated in rabbinic lore: It happened once that R. Reuben was in Tiberius on the Sabbath, and a philosopher asked him: 'Who is the most hateful man in the world?' He replied, 'The man who denies his Creator.' 'How so?', said the philosopher. R. Reuben answered, 'Honour thy father and thy mother, thou shalt do no murder, thou shalt not commit adultery, thou shalt not steal, thou shalt not bear false witness against thy neighbour, thou shalt not covet.' No man denies the derivative (that is, the separate commandments) until he has previously denied the Root (that is, God), and no man sins unless he has denied him who commanded him not to commit that sin.

Moral precepts are grounded in the will of God; in this light the Torah serves as the blueprint for moral action, and it is through the admonitions of the rabbis in midrashic and Talmudic sources that the Jewish people are encouraged to put the teachings of the law into effect in their everyday life. In the hierarchy of values, the rabbis declared that justice is of fundamental importance. Rabbi Simeon b. Gamaliel, for example, remarked: 'Do not sneer at justice, for it is one of the three feet of the world, for the sages taught that the world stands on three things: justice, truth and peace.' According to Rabbi Elazar:

the whole Torah depends upon justice. Therefore God gave enactments about justice immediately after the Ten Commandments, because men transgress justice, and God punishes them, and He teaches the inhabitants of the world. Sodom was not overthrown till the men of Sodom neglected justice, and the men of Jerusalem were not banished till they disregarded justice.

In explaining what is entailed in the principle of justice, the rabbis explained what is required in a court of law. With reference to the Deuteronomic injunction, 'Thou shalt not take a bribe, for a bribe blinds the eyes of the wise', Rabbi Hama b. Osha'ya stated: 'If a man suffers from his eyes, he pays much money to a doctor, but it is doubtful whether he will be healed or not. But he who takes a bribe overturns justice, blinds his eyes, brings Israel into exile, and hunger into the modern world.' Regarding the statement in Leviticus, 'In righteousness shalt thou judge thy neighbour', the Sifra proclaims: 'You must not let one litigant speak as much as he wants, and then say to the other, "shorten thy speech." You must not let one stand and the other sit.' Rabbi Simeon b. Shetach said:

> When you are judging, and there come before you two men, of whom one is rich and the other poor, do not say, 'the poor man's words are to be believed, but not the rich man's.' But just as you listen to the words of the poor man, listen to the words of the rich man, for it is said, 'Ye shall not respect persons in judgement.'

THE DISTINCTIVE NATURE OF JEWISH SOCIAL ETHICS

According to rabbinic literature, the Kingdom of God is inextricably linked to the establishment of a moral order on earth. For the Jewish people the Kingdom of God is inconsistent with injustice and social misery; the effort to bring about the perfection of the world so that God will reign in majesty is a human responsibility. Jewish ethics as enshrined in the Bible and in rabbinic literature are inextricably related to the coming of God's Kingdom. In this context a number of distinctive characteristics of Jewish morality are expressed in the Jewish tradition.

First, as we have seen in connection with the prophets, there was an intensity of passion about the moral demands made upon human beings. For sins of personal greed, social inequity, and deceit, the prophet in God's name denounced the people and threatened horrific catastrophes. The voice of the prophet was continually charged with agony and agitation. Habakkuk, for example, declared:

> Woe to him who heaps up what is not his own . . .
> Woe to him who gets evil gain for his house . . .
> For the stone will cry out from the wall,
> and the beam from the woodwork respond.
> Woe to him who builds a town with blood,
> and founds a city on iniquity! (Hab. 2.6, 9, 11–12).

Such shrill denunciations of iniquity were the result of the prophetic conviction that people must be stirred from their spiritual slumber. 'The prophet's word is a scream in the night . . . while the world is at ease and asleep, the prophet feels the blast from heaven.'[4]

Second, Jewish ethics required that each person be treated equally. Biblical and rabbinic sources show a constant concern to eliminate arbitrary distinctions between individuals so as to establish a proper balance between competing claims. On the basis of the biblical view that everyone is created in the image of God, the Torah declared that false and irrelevant distinctions must not be introduced to disqualify human beings from the right to justice. The fatherhood and motherhood of God implied human solidarity; the Torah rejected the idea of different codes of morality for oneself and others, for the great and the humbled, for rulers and ruled, for individuals and nations, for private and public citizens. Given this understanding of the equality of all people, the Torah singled out the underprivileged and the defenceless in society for consideration: 'You shall not afflict any widow or orphan' (Exod. 22.22); 'you shall not be partial to the poor or defer to the great' (Lev. 19.15).

Since all of humanity is created in the image of God, Judaism maintains that there is no fundamental difference between Jew and non-Jew: God's ethical demands apply to all. In the Midrash we read: 'This is the gate of the Lord into which the righteous shall enter: not priest, Levites, or Israelites, but the righteous, though they be non-Jews' (Sifra, Acharei mot, 13). Indeed, according to the Talmud, the righteous non-Jew was accorded a place in the hereafter: 'The pious of all nations have a share in the world to come' (San. 105a). In this light, the rabbis emphasized that Jews must treat their non-Jewish neighbours with loving-kindness. One of the most authoritative rabbis of the last century declared:

> It is well known that the early as well as the later geonim wrote that we must abide by the law of the land and refrain from dealing unjustly with a non-Jew . . . Therefore, my brethren, listen to my voice and live. Study in our Torah to love the Almighty and love people regardless of faith or nationality. Follow justice and do righteousness with Jew and non-Jew alike. The people of my community know that I always caution them in my talks and warn them that there is absolutely no difference whether one does evil to a Jew or a non-Jew. It is a well-known fact that when people come to me to settle a dispute, I do not differentiate between Jew and non-Jew. For that is the law according to our holy Torah.[5]

A third characteristic of Jewish morality is its emphasis on human motivation. The Jewish faith is not solely concerned with actions and their consequences; it also demands right intention. The rabbis explained: 'The Merciful One requires the heart' (San. 106b). It is true that Judaism emphasized the importance of moral action, but the Jewish faith also focuses attention on right-mindedness: inner experiences – motives, feelings, dispositions, and attitudes – are of supreme moral significance. For this reason the rabbis identified a group of negative commandments in the Torah involving thought. The following are representative examples:

> Thou shalt not take vengeance, nor bear any grudge against the children of thy people (Lev. 19.18).
> There are six things which the Lord hates . . . a heart that devises wicked plans (Prov. 6.16, 18).
> Take heed last there be a base thought in your heart (Deut. 15.9).

In the Mishnah the rabbis elaborated on this concern for the human heart:

> Rabbi Eliezer said, '. . . be not easily moved to anger' (Avot 2.15).
> Rabbi Joshua said, 'The evil eye, the evil inclination, and hatred of his fellow creatures drives a man out of the world' (Avot 2.16).
> Rabbi Levitas of Yavneh said, 'Be exceedingly lowly of spirit' (Avot 2.16).

Connected with right thought is the Jewish emphasis on right speech. Jewish sources insist that individuals are morally responsible for the words they utter. Proverbs declared: 'Death and life are in the power of the tongue' (Prov. 18.21). Evil words spoken about one person by another could arouse hatred and enmity and destroy human relations. The rabbis considered slander to be a particular evil: 'Whoever speaks slander is as though he denied the fundamental principle [existence of God]. The Holy One, blessed be He, says of such a person who speaks slander, "I and he cannot dwell together in the world"' (Pe'ah 15d, Areakh in 15b). There was also a positive aspect to this emphasis on human speech. Just as the rabbis condemned false utterances, they urged their disciples to offer cheerful greetings (Avot 1.15; 3.16, 12). Anger could be soothed with gentle words and reconciliation could be brought about.[4]

A fourth dimension of Jewish morality concerns the traditional attitude towards animals. Since God's mercy and goodness extend to all creatures (Ps. 145.9), 'A righteous man has regard for the life of his beast' (Prov. 12.10). According to Jewish tradition, human beings are morally obliged to refrain from inflicting pain on animals. The Pentateuch stipulated that assistance be given to animals in distress even on the Sabbath: 'You shall not see your brother's ass or his ox fallen down by the way, and withhold your help from them; you shall help him to lift them up again' (Deut. 22.4). In rabbinic Judaism this same theme was reflected in various midrashim. We read, for example, concerning Rabbi Judah Ha Nasi:

> Rabbi Judah was sitting studying the Torah in front of the Babylonian synagogue in Sepphoris, when a calf passed before him on its way to the slaughter and began to cry out as though pleading, 'Save me!' Said he to it, 'What can I do for you? For this you were created.' As a punishment for his heartlessness, he suffered toothache for thirteen years. One day, a weasel ran past his daughter, who was about to kill it, when he said to her, 'My daughter, let it be, for it is written, "and His tender mercies are over all His works." ' Because the Rabbi prevented an act of cruelty, he was once again restored to health (Baba Metzia, 85a).

A final aspect of Jewish ethics is their concern for human dignity; Judaism puts a strong emphasis on the respect due to all individuals. This concept was found in various laws in the Pentateuch and was developed by the rabbis who cautioned that one must be careful not to humiliate or embarrass others. Maimonides, for example, wrote:

> A man ought to be especially heedful of his behaviour towards widows and orphans, for their souls are exceedingly depressed and their spirits low, even if they are wealthy. How are we to conduct ourselves toward them? One must not speak to them otherwise than tenderly. One must show them unvarying courtesy; not hurt them physically with hard toil nor wound their feelings with harsh speech (Hilchot De'ot 6.10).

The Torah's concern for human dignity even included thieves. Rabbi Yochanan b. Zakai pointed out that according to the law whoever stole a sheep should pay a fine of four times the value of the sheep; whoever stole an ox must pay five times its value. Those who stole sheep had to undergo the embarrassment for this indignity, but those who stole oxen were spared such embarrassment because they could simply lead the ox by its tether (Baba Kamma 99b).

These specific qualities of Jewish ethics illustrate their humane orientation to all of God's creatures. Throughout biblical and rabbinic literature Jews were encouraged to strive for the highest conception of life, in which the rule of truth, righteousness, and holiness would be established among humankind. Such a desire is the eternal hope of God's people.

THE FOCUS ON MORAL ACTION

As we have seen, the Jewish hope for the future lies in God's sovereign rule on earth. From ancient times the synagogue liturgy concluded with a prayer in which this hope was expressed:

May we speedily behold the glory of Thy might,
when Thou wilt remove the abomination from the earth,
and the idols will be utterly cut off;
when the world will be perfected under the kingdom of the Almighty,
and all the children of flesh will call upon Thy name;
when Thou wilt turn unto Thyself all the wicked of the earth.

This is the goal of the history of the world in which God's chosen people have a central role. In this context the people of Israel have a historical mission to be a light to the nations. Through Moses God addressed the people and declared:

You have seen what I did to the Egyptians, and how I bore you on eagles' wings and brought you to myself. Now therefore, if you will obey my voice and keep my covenant, you shall be my own possession among all peoples; for all the earth is mine, and you shall be to me a kingdom of priests and a holy nation (Exod. 19.4–6).

Election meant to be a servant of the Lord, to proclaim God's truth and righteousness throughout the world. Being chosen meant duty and responsibility; it was 'a divine call persisting through all ages and encompassing all lands, a continuous activity of the spirit which has ever summoned for itself new heralds and heroes to testify to truth, justice and sublime faith'.[6]

Judaism did not separate religion from life; instead Jews were called to action, to turn humankind away from violence, wickedness and falsehood. It was not the hope of bliss in a future life but the establishment of the kingdom of justice and peace that was central to the Jewish faith. Moral praxis was at the heart of the religious tradition. The people of Israel as a light to the nations reflected the moral nature of God; each Jew was to be like the Creator, mirroring the divine qualities revealed to Moses: 'The Lord, the Lord, a God merciful and gracious, slow to anger, and abounding in steadfast love and faithfulness, keeping steadfast love for thousands, forgiving iniquity and transgression and sin' (Exod. 34.6–7).

God as a moral being demanded righteous living, as the Psalms declared: 'the Lord is righteous, he loves righteous deeds' (Ps. 11.7); 'righteousness and justice are the foundation of his throne' (Ps. 97.2); 'thou hast established equity; thou hast executed justice and righteousness' (Ps. 99.4). Given this theological framework, Jews were directed to obey the revealed will of God, which was the basis of the covenantal relationship between God and the Jewish nation. Orthopraxis, rather than conceptual reflection, served as the foundation of the religion of Israel.

In the Bible, deeds and events involving moral issues could be found in abundance: the punishment of Cain for murdering his brother, the violence of the generation that brought on the Flood, the early prohibition against murder, the hospitality of Abraham and his pleading for the people of Sodom, the praise of Abraham for his moral attitudes, the condemnation of Joseph's brothers, Joseph's self-restraint in the house of Potiphar, Moses' intercessions on the side of the exploited.[7]

But it is pre-eminently in the legal codes of the Pentateuch that we encounter moral guidelines formulated in specific rules. The Decalogue in particular illustrates the centrality of moral praxis in the life of the Jew. The first four commandments are theological in character, but the last six deal with relationships between human beings. The first commandment describes God as one who redeemed the Jews from Egypt; the one who forbade the worship of other deities and demanded respect for the Sabbath and the divine name. These commandments were expressions of the love and fear of God; the remaining injunctions provided a means of expressing love of other human beings. The Decalogue made it clear that moral rules were fundamental to the Jewish faith.

Such ethical standards were repeated in the prophetic books. The teachings of the prophets were rooted in the Torah of Moses. The prophets saw themselves as messengers of the divine word; their special task was to denounce the people for their transgressions and call them to repentance. In all this they pointed to concrete action – moral praxis – as the only means of sustaining the covenantal relationship with God. The essential theme of their message was that God demanded righteousness and justice.

Emphasis on the moral life was reflected in the prophetic condemnation of cultural practices that were not accompanied by ethical concern. These passages illustrated that ritual commandments were of instrumental value; morality was intrinsic and absolute. The primacy of morality was also reflected in the prophetic warning that righteous action was the determining factor in the destiny of the Jewish nation. Moral transgressions referred to in such contexts concerned exploitation, oppression and the perversion of justice. These sins had the potential to bring about the downfall of the nation.

The book of Proverbs reinforced the teaching of the Torah and the prophets; wisdom was conceived here as the capacity to act morally; it was a skill that could be learnt. Throughout Proverbs dispositional traits and moral types were listed: This suggests that moral virtue or vice is to be achieved not by concentrating on individual moral acts but rather by learning to recognise and emulate certain good personality types. Thus here, as in the rest of the Bible, the moral life was seen as the foundation of the Jewish faith. Theology was defined in relation to practical activity; it was through ethical praxis that humanity encountered the divine.

Rabbinic literature continued this emphasis on action. Convinced they were the authentic expositors of Scripture, the rabbis amplified biblical law. In their expansion of the commandments, rabbinic exegetes differentiated between the laws governing human relationships to God (*bain adam la makom*) and those that concerned human relationships to others (*bain adam le chavero*). As in the biblical period, rabbinic teachings reflected the same sense of the primacy of morality. Such texts as the following indicated rabbinic priority:

> He who acts honestly and is popular with his fellow creatures, it is imputed to him as though he had fulfilled the entire Torah (Mekhilta on Exodus 15.26).
> Hillel said: 'What is hateful to yourself, do not do to your fellow man. This is the entire Torah, the rest is commentary' (Shabbat 31a).
> Better is one hour of repentance and good deeds in this world than the whole life of the world-to-come (Avot 4.22).

In the classic texts of Judaism, then, moral behaviour was the predominant theme. By choosing the moral life, the Jew could help to complete God's work of creation. To accomplish this task the rabbis formulated an elaborate system of traditions, which were written down in the Mishnah, subsequently expanded in the Talmud, and eventually codified in the *Code of Jewish Law*. According to traditional Judaism, this expansion of the Pentateuchal law was part of God's revelation. Both the written law (*Torah Shebikthav*) and the oral law (*Torah Shebe-'alpe*) were binding on Jews for all time:

> The Torah has been revealed from Heaven. This implies our belief that the whole of the Torah found in our hands this day is the Torah that was handed down by Moses and that it is all of divine origin. By this I mean that the whole of the Torah came unto him from before God in a manner which is metaphorically called speaking.[8]

Since the Torah embraced the Pentateuch as well as its traditional interpretation, orthodoxy maintained that God gave to Moses the laws in the Pentateuch as well as their explanations:

> The verse: 'And I will give thee the tables of stone, and the Law and the commandment, which I have written that thou mayest teach them' (Ex. 24:12) means as follows: 'The tables of stone' are the ten commandments; 'the law' is the Pentateuch; 'the commandment' is the Mishnah; 'which I have written' are the Prophets and the Hagiographa; 'that thou mayest teach them' is the Gemara (Talmud). This teaches that all these things were given on Sinai.[8]

Given this view of the Torah, Jews regarded the moral law as absolute and binding. In all cases the law was precise and specific; it was God's word made concrete in the daily life of the Jew. The commandment to love one's neighbours embraced all humanity. In the *Code of Jewish Law* the virtues of justice, honesty and humane concern were regarded as central virtues of community life; hatred, vengeance, deceit, cruelty and anger were condemned as antisocial. The Jew was instructed to exercise loving-kindness towards all: to clothe the naked, to feed the hungry, to care for the sick, and to comfort the mourner. By fulfilling these ethical demands, the Jewish people could bring about God's Kingdom on earth, in which exploitation, oppression and injustice would be eliminated. What was required in this task was a commitment to ethical praxis as a policy.

These aspects of the Jewish heritage – the Exodus experience, the prophetic message, the doctrine of the Kingdom of God, the nature of Jewish ethics, and the focus on moral action – point the way to a sympathetic appreciation of the plight of those who are afflicted in modern society.

THE JEWISH RESPONSE TO MODERN INNER-CITY PROBLEMS

The biblical and rabbinic traditions portray God's reign on earth as the goal of mankind – a world in which all people shall turn away from iniquity, injustice and oppression. This is not the hope of bliss in a future life, but the building up of the divine Kingdom of truth and peace for all. By putting themselves in the shoes of the disadvantaged – thereby recalling their own history of suffering – the Jewish community can envisage what life must be for the underprivileged.

Such a policy of caring and sharing based on biblical and rabbinic sources transcends the much narrower prescriptions of the Chief Rabbi. Lord Jakobovits is correct when he declares that Judaism recommends education, diligence and hard work as one solution to individual poverty. Yet the Jewish people have had a wider vision in the past. There have been other virtues besides self-reliance, such as justice, compassion, charity and sympathy. The recommendations of the Chief Rabbi are not merely an unrealistic solution to the problems of our inner cities, they also belie the richness and fullness of the Jewish heritage. The Jewish teachings we have surveyed focus on the traditional commitment to those who are downtrodden. In the past such prescriptions were directed primarily to Jewry itself, since Jews lived in closed communities with relatively little contact with the non-Jewish world. Today all this has changed. In the modern world Jews have become full citizens of the countries in which they dwell and are assimilated into contemporary society. Such altered circumstances should provide the basis for a Jewish commitment to all those who are downtrodden and marginalized, whatever their race or religion.

As God's suffering servant through the ages, the Jewish people should find solidarity with today's poor of paramount significance. The prophets condemned every kind of abuse. Scripture speaks of positive action to prevent poverty from becoming widespread. Leviticus and Deuteronomy contain detailed legislation designed to prevent the accumulation of wealth and consequent exploitation of the unfortunate. Now that the ghettos have disappeared, modern Jews should feel an obligation to take steps to eradicate poverty and suffering wherever it exists. In particular, they should address themselves to the economic deprivation that affects certain groups: the young, who are frustrated by the lack of opportunity to obtain training and work; manual labourers, who are frequently ill-paid and find difficulty in defending their rights; the unemployed, who are discarded because of the harsh exigencies of economic life; and the old, who are often marginalized and disregarded. In all such cases, the Jewish people – who have consistently endured hardship – should feel drawn to the downtrodden of modern society, sharing in their distress.

In attempting to accomplish this task, the plight of those living in the inner cities is of central importance. Here the distinction between the powerful and the powerless is most clearly evident. In the cities – as opposed to the suburbs – are to be found the unemployed, families unable to cope, single parents, people with only part-time jobs, individuals on welfare, drop-outs, and recent immigrants. In such areas inhabitants are divorced from the powerful forces that shape their lives: the inner city is the place of failure and hopelessness. The graphic social divide between the rich and the poor is an everyday reality for those who live in large metropolitan centres. All too often the poverty of the inner city is the converse side of middle-class suburban life. The situation of the poor is an integral part of the elaborate hierarchy of wealth and esteem. The existence of rich suburbs is linked to the existence of ghettos and marginal sectors. A new consciousness is needed to remedy this situation, an awareness of the calamities of inner-city deprivation. By ministering to those at the bottom of society, Jews can affirm through their efforts that God is concerned with the plight of those facing adversity. In the inner city Jews can embark on a task of reconstruction and restoration.

In this connection, special attention should be paid to the situation of the unemployed who are generally found in the destitute parts of the inner city. Such individuals face particular difficulties in coping with

131

their misfortunes. The unemployed do not know what to do with their time, and as a consequence they are unfulfilled in essential areas: basic human needs for human relationships, for financial income, for social status and identity, and for satisfaction and fulfilment. Helping those faced with such difficulties should be a high priority. The Jewish community can take the lead in assisting those out of work. Recently several writers have made a number of suggestions about the kinds of activities that could be undertaken: ways must be sought for creating new work opportunities; labour not traditionally regarded as paid work (such as housework) must be accepted as valid and necessary; new manufacturing enterprises that stimulate the job market should be encouraged; apprenticeships for the young should be reintroduced; jobs need to be spread out through job sharing and part-time work; education must be seen as a preparation for life; voluntary activity should be stimulated and seen as a legitimate means of helping those in need.

In the quest to alleviate distress and disillusionment, Jews can make substantial contributions to those at the bottom of the social scale. Liberation from frustration and disappointment involves a reappraisal of life and labour: it is a task that can bind together the Jewish community in the quest for a meaningful life for all.

Notes

1 The article appeared in the issue of 24 January 1986. All subsequent quotations used in this essay are taken from there.
2 Subsequent quotations from the Passover service that are used in this essay have been taken from *The Union Haggadah* (UAHC, 1923).
3 S. Schechter, *Aspects of Rabbinic Theology* (Schechter, 1961), p. 93.
4 A. J. Heschel, *The Prophets* (New York, Harper & Row, 1955), p. 16.
5 I. Spektor, 'Nachal Yitzchak' in S. Spero (ed.), *Morality, Halakha and the Jewish Tradition* (Hoboken NJ, KTAV Press, 1983), p. 134.
6 K. Kohler, *Jewish Theology* (Hoboken NJ, KTAV Press, 1968), p. 326.
7 S. Spero, *Morality, Halakha and the Jewish Tradition*, p. 22.
8 Maimonides, as quoted in L. Jacobs, *Principles of the Jewish Faith* (Vallentine Mitchell, 1964), p. 216.
9 R. Levi b. Hama, in the name of R. Simeon b. Laquish, quoted in ibid., p. 282.